SURVIVING THE NOT SO GOLDEN YEARS

Vital Medical and Financial Strategies
for Anyone Planning to Grow Old

SURVIVING
THE
NOT SO GOLDEN YEARS

Vital Medical and Financial Strategies for Anyone Planning to Grow Old

M. Therese Young

SHAPOLSKY PUBLISHERS, INC.

NEW YORK

A Shapolsky Book

Copyright © 1991 by M. Therese Young

All rights reserved under International and Pan American Copyright conventions. Published in the U.S.A. by Shapolsky Publishers, Inc. No parts of this book may be used or reproduced in any manner whatsoever without written permission of Shapolsky Publishers, Inc., except in the case of brief quotations embodied in critical articles or reviews.

For any additional information, contact:
Shapolsky Publishers, Inc.
136 West 22nd Street
New York NY 10011
(212) 633-2022

10 9 8 7 6 5 4 3 2 1

ISBN 1-56171-005-9

Design and Typography by Sally Ann Zegarelli
Long Branch, NJ 07740

Printed and bound by Graficromo s.a., Cordoba, Spain

To my mother

ACKNOWLEDGMENTS

I wish to express my appreciation to the following people for their contribution to this project:

To my husband, Paul Tedesco, for his belief in the importance of the project and for his unfailing patience through it all. To my dad for his positive attitude and for always being there for me. To my sister Ann for helping streamline my initial draft. To my stepchildren Carolyn, Kathy, and John for their boundless enthusiasm and moral support. To my friends Joan, Nancy, and Judy for their endless encouragement. And to Janice for always making the time to listen to one more question or hear one more idea.

I would also like to thank my editor, Ann Cassouto, whose skillful guidance and invaluable suggestions were critical to the successful completion of this project. And thanks also go to my agent, Merrill Cohen, whose initial contribution was the key to making this book possible.

Writing the book would have been an impossible task without the able assistance and cooperation of the individual professionals who work in the Medicaid offices in each state. Specifically, I would like to express my special gratitude to Mike Stevens of the Department of Health and Rehabilitative Services in Sarasota, Florida. His kindness, patience, and sensitivity to my lack of awareness of all that was entailed in resolving my mother's situation made an arduous and overwhelming task much simpler and less stressful to cope with.

CONTENTS

INTRODUCTION: *Why Read This Book?* xiii

PART ONE—MEDICAID AND LONG-TERM
    HEALTH CARE 1

    Chapter 1: *One Out of One Hundred and Eighty* 3

        Medicare 4

        Medicaid 5

    Chapter 2: *The Consequences of Ignorance* 10

        Rose and Joe Sider 10

        Anne and Jack Fleming 13

        Mother's Story 15

    Chapter 3: *Basic Information on Medicaid* 19

        Eligibility Requirements 19

        Information on Income and Resource
            Considerations 20

        Basic, or "Usual," Exemptions from Countable
            Resources 22

        The Transfer of Assets for Eligibility
            Requirements 23

        The Medicare Catastrophic Health Bill as It
            Affects Medicaid Regulations 23

        General Information on Applying for Medicaid 24

Chapter 4: *Medicaid Information State by State* 26

    Basic Eligibility Requirements, Addresses,
        and Telephone Numbers 26

PART TWO—LONG-TERM HEALTH CARE
FACILITIES 77

    Chapter 5: *Why It Is Important for You to Know About
        Nursing Home Facilities* 79

        When and Why You Should Consider a Nursing
            Home Facility 80

        Issues to Consider When Selecting a Nursing
            Home Facility 82

    Chapter 6: *Important Facts That You Should Know* 86

        Basic Facts About Nursing Homes 86

        Nursing Home Policies Toward Medicaid State
            by State 88

    Chapter 7: *Other Options* 131

        "I Didn't Know Help Was Available" 131

PART THREE—FINANCIAL CONSIDERATIONS 139

    Chapter 8: *Protecting Your Assets* 141

        Family Situations That Should Flag Potential
            Financial Problems 141

        Basic Steps for Assessing Your Own or Someone
            Else's Financial Position 142

        Options for Spending Down—Should It Be
            Necessary 144

CONTENTS

Why and When to Seek Professional Advice in
   Planning Your Financial Assets Protection 145

Issues to Raise in Order to Determine the
   Qualifications of the Professional You Choose .. 148

PART FOUR—DIRECTORY OF GOVERNMENT
   REPRESENTATIVES 151

Chapter 9: *You* Can *Make a Difference* 153

Guidelines for Corresponding with Government
   Officials 154

Samples of Correspondence 155

Names, Addresses, and Telephone Numbers of
   Members of Congress and of Governors 159

AFTERWORD 193

GLOSSARY 195

APPENDIX: *Some Vital Statistics* 199

INTRODUCTION: WHY READ THIS BOOK?

During the next few years, one out of every 180 people living in this country will face the immediate crisis of having to live in a nursing home. Their families will have to deal with the myriad questions, frustrating lack of information and assistance, as well as, eventually, the prohibitive costs of that nursing home.

The information contained in this book is intended to help simplify all of these tasks, and to do so, I begin in Part One by covering a relatively revolutionary concept which can alleviate the financial burden—that concept being Medicaid, as an alternative solution to financial disaster for middle-class families facing this dilemma. For example, in the instance of long-term health care for the aged, only the recipient of Medicaid, *not* the spouse, must be close to impoverishment to be financially eligible for Medicaid. This is the rule in all but a very few states. And as of October 1989, that portion of the new Catastrophic Health Bill which protects the spouses of Medicaid recipients from impoverishment goes into effect in all states.

Part Two deals with facts about nursing homes that are related to Medicaid. The fact is, only a very few nursing homes in each state are run by the state or county. The overwhelming majority of nursing homes in all states are privately owned and operated. Almost all of these nursing homes participate in Medicaid—and do so in order to remain financially solvent.

Also, there are some practices that currently exist in some nursing homes which are in direct violation of the federal regulations governing Medicaid. These violations are cited. Finally, for each state, listed on a per diem and annual basis, is the average cost of a private nursing home subscribing to Medicaid.

Part Three specifically spells out the need for financial asset planning and protection, particularly when the possibility of a health care crisis can be anticipated. It does so in a vernacular that is both palatable and easy to read. It also dispels the theory that asset protection should emanate only from the lofty libraries of the esteemed lawyers of the upper class. Financial protection is no longer the exclusive domain of society's affluent but a practical necessity for anyone who has managed to accumulate any assets.

This book came about as a result of a personal experience. In 1987 my mother was diagnosed as having Alzheimer's disease and had to be confined to a nursing home for her remaining years. It was during this period, when I so desperately needed the above information, that I discovered it was nowhere to be found. Neither health professionals, social workers, agencies for the aged, books, nor publications were of much help. I myself did not feel emotionally equipped, nor did I have the desire, to plow through the ponderous material that was available on long-term health care. As for Medicaid, there was and still is, to the best of my knowledge, no existing compendium of the above information. Any commercial reading material available either misrepresented the facts on Medicaid and nursing homes or touched so briefly on Medicaid as to be considered a last, desperate measure.

The facts contained in this book were carefully researched over the last two years through interviews, numerous and extensive phone calls, plus correspondence to all the appropriate people in the appropriate agencies, in order to establish and verify certain key facts as well as give all the information provided. The material is presented in a clear, simple, "bottom line" style, affording the reader the most definitive and critical information with the least amount of effort.

INTRODUCTION: WHY READ THIS BOOK?

Finally, I feel the information contained in the book is in a manner of speaking "consciousness raising" material, to the extent that most middle-class people know very little about the differences between Medicare and Medicaid. They know even less about Medicaid, believing it is a program for indigent or welfare recipients only. As we have experienced it, this is no longer true. The information presented here should be of interest to anyone who is in any way associated with someone facing the necessity of going into a long-term health care facility, whether family or friend. It is no longer data to be used exclusively by health professionals, government agency employees, or personnel in the medical field, but information that should be made available to the general public. This book provides that service.

PART ONE

Medicaid and Long-Term Health Care

Chapter 1

ONE OUT OF ONE HUNDRED AND EIGHTY

Do you know this person? Could this person be you or someone close to you? Statistics show that by the year 1990, one out of every 180 people living in this country will be a permanent resident in a nursing home. About 1.5 million[1] people will fall into this category.

This category unfortunately does not consist of just a select group in our society whose numbers will eventually dwindle down. On the contrary, this category is a cross-section of our society that includes all ethnic, religious, and racial segments without discrimination. It is a category which is statistically on the rise due to the incidence of Alzheimer's disease and other illnesses associated with the aging process. Medical and technological science, too, has prolonged life beyond the point where people can adequately take care of themselves.

Unless you can guarantee that these statistics will never affect your life, you owe it to yourself to read the next few paragraphs and to investigate the information contained in this

---

[1] *Aging America*, U.S. Administration on Aging, and 1985 National Nursing Home Survey.

book. It could be very critical at some time in your life. For many of you, it could mean saving hundreds, thousands, tens of thousands, or hundreds of thousands of dollars over a period of a few years. Money that could be yours, your parents' or a close relative's.

Just ask yourself the following questions:

- Do I know for certain that, neither I, nor my spouse, nor my parents will ever be in need of a long-term care or a nursing home facility?
- Will health insurance or Medicare cover this expense if the person in the facility can't afford to pay?
- If someone goes into a long-term health care facility permanently, what will be the annual cost for the facility?
- Do I know the difference between Medicare and Medicaid?
- What is Medicaid?
- Who is financially eligible for Medicaid?
- Are all the regulations governing Medicaid interpreted and administered uniformly throughout the states or do they differ from state to state?

If you were unable to answer these questions, then consider that

(1) contrary to the belief held by over 70% of the population, Medicare does not absorb the long-term cost of a nursing home facility; and
(2) almost all private insurance companies without exception, do *not* cover the extended cost of long-term health care/nursing home facilities.

MEDICARE

Medicare is actually Title XVIII of the Social Security Act enacted into law in 1966. It is basically a program run by the federal government through the Department of Health and Human Services, formerly known as the Social Security Administration. To be eligible for Medicare you must be 65 years old or older and eligible for Social Security. It is a type of Federal Health Insurance and, as with all insurance, it has premiums, deductibles and co-insurance. When you subscribe to Medicare you are automatically enrolled in PART A (below). And for most people there is no premium for PART A. PART B, or SMI (Supplemental Medical Insurance) (below), however, is optional and carries a monthly premium.

> PART A covers (for a *limited time only*): Hospital costs for inpatient care; skilled nursing facility care; hospice care; home health care.
> PART B covers: Doctors' services; outpatient hospital service, and some other health care services not covered in PART A.

MEDICAID

"Medicaid is a program that pays bills for low income people who cannot afford the cost of Health Care." This is a direct quote from a government pamphlet on Medicaid which not only is oversimplified but is most definitely, in part, misleading.

Medicaid is a federal program, also known as Title XIX of the Social Security Act enacted into law in 1966. Medicaid is funded only by your and my tax dollars for the sole purpose of helping to mitigate or absorb the rising and exorbitant medical expenses of those who cannot pay. It is a program which functions in tandem with state funds, which are also derived from your and my tax dollars, and it is administered by each state under the guidelines and regulations determined by the federal government.

In a broader sense, Medicaid can probably be considered a type of Federal Medical Insurance Program into which all taxpayers must contribute. And even though, as with all medical insurance, we hope we never have cause to draw on it, Medicaid is there for us to rightfully use should unfortunate circumstances necessitate our doing so. *It is most certainly NOT TAKING A HAND-OUT!*

Unfortunately, due to the prohibitive costs of long-term health care, the category of Medicaid subscribers is no longer limited to those with low incomes and the indigent. Today, Medicaid is fast becoming the only option available to middle-

SURVIVING THE NOT SO GOLDEN YEARS

income families when one family member faces the prospect of having to reside permanently in a long-term health care facility and that one member is financially unable to pay the costs.

Consider the following:

The average cost of a private nursing home/long-term health care facility in the United States is approximately $25,000 a year, or in some urban areas up to $60,000 a year. If a person enters a nursing home/long-term health care facility at the age of seventy-two, because he or she can no longer care for him or herself, and he or she lives to the age of eighty-five, the cost of their nursing home/long-term health care facility will over thirteen years be at least $325,000, or as high as $780,000. These projected figures assume there will be no increase in the cost of long-term health care during that period of time. How many families can support that kind of health care—regardless of how much someone is loved?

Armed with these startling and overwhelming figures and the knowledge that only through the Medicaid program can most middle-income families handle this type of cost, you should at least familiarize yourself with the rules governing Medicaid as it applies to long-term health care/nursing home facilities and as it is administered by your state.

Although Medicaid is a federal program, each state interprets the regulations according to its own needs and each state administers its funding differently. There are some basic regulations and these will be covered later, but first let us examine the "why" of the need to know.

Unfortunately, whether you are young adults, mature adults, or senior citizens, there is no way of knowing when the need for long-term health care or a nursing home facility will be necessary for someone very close to you or for that matter, yourself. When this need arises, having a knowledge of the necessary requirements for being accepted into Medicaid can make the difference between being able to hold your own financially in the face of catastrophic costs or being totally impoverished.

When the need for Medicaid arises, the information is not always readily accessible. Either you must go to some Social Service Agency and wade through the lines of people, or you must write to the appropriate government organization for

MEDICAID AND LONG-TERM HEALTH CARE

information and then wait until you receive a response, or go to the nearest library and hope that you can locate the books or pamphlets containing the necessary information. In all cases you must figuratively plow through a maze of "Federalese and legalese," looking up the regulations and referring to coded sections of the regulations, often working your way through mounds of extraneous material before coming to the information which pertains to your situation.

This book is not intended to be a synopsis of all the regulations governing Medicaid in all the fifty states and covering all categories. That would be somewhat analogous to writing "The History of the World" and attempting to condense it into a pamphlet. Realistically trying to condense all the regulations covering the numerous aspects of Medicaid would be an impossible task. What this book does cover is as follows:

Part One provides the readers with information for each state regarding:

- basic regulations, which determine eligibility for Medicaid in the aged category, as applied to long-term health care/nursing home facilities; also included are the new guidelines as provided by the Medicare Catastrophic Coverage Act
- names, addresses, and telephone numbers of Medicaid offices in each state, which can provide more extensive information regarding your individual concerns
- basic information, including a list of the appropriate documents required to apply for Medicaid

This information is presented in a clear and easy to understand format that enables the reader to compare benefits and requirements for each of the fifty states, and will give a sense of how Medicaid relates to his or her particular situation.

Part Two provides the reader with the following:

- a list of issues which anyone who will ever need the services of a nursing home for themselves or a loved one should know, including where to begin to find a suitable nursing home, assuming you know absolutely nothing about this subject

SURVIVING THE NOT SO GOLDEN YEARS

- basic facts concerning private (as opposed to state-operated) nursing homes in each of the fifty states (the majority of nursing homes in each state, as in at least nine out of ten, are private)
- the telephone numbers to call for further information on nursing homes in each of the fifty states

Part Three briefly highlights some circumstances that should alert people to the possibility of economic problems:

- the single person who is anticipating a long-term health care facility at some time in the near future
- the couple who lives with the knowledge that one of them will probably have to go into a long-term health care facility sometime in the very near future
- the single person who is in immediate need of long-term health care and financial assistance
- the couple who, besides knowing that one of them is in immediate need of a long-term health care facility, also knows they will immediately need financial assistance

Also provided are some hints that could prove useful in:

- evaluating the financial situation of the persons in the above circumstances
- some considerations for establishing a strategy or plan for protecting any or all of the assets of the person or persons involved in the above situations

The second part of Part Three looks at:

- the feasibility and advantages of engaging a qualified attorney or financial advisor to handle and help plan your financial future versus the disadvantages in trying to "do it yourself"
- some issues and questions to raise with an attorney or financial advisor that may help to satisfy any concerns you have as to the qualifications of the person you have chosen

MEDICAID AND LONG-TERM HEALTH CARE

Part Four includes the following:

- guidelines for corresponding with government representatives and officials
- samples of correspondence
- names, telephone numbers, and the local addresses of all the senators and representatives of each state
- names and addresses of the residences (home and official) for the governors of each state

Chapter 2

THE CONSEQUENCES OF IGNORANCE

ROSE AND JOE SIDER

Rose and Joe Sider are an average retired couple. Joe is 72 and Rose is 70. Joe is retired from his civil service job with the state and is collecting a pension of about $15,000 a year. Rose and Joe live in a comfortable home worth about $100,000 and own a nice car worth about $7,500. Joe and Rose have three married children, Sarah, Michael, and Ellen, who live in Los Angeles, Chicago, and Boston respectively.

Rose and Joe are currently living in Indianapolis, Indiana, and have considered moving to Florida but have put it off each year because they wanted to stay close to at least one of their children.

Rose and Joe over the years managed to save a nice nest egg of about $75,000, which they wanted to enjoy in their "Golden Years" for traveling, etc. Also, they felt pretty secure in the fact that they were both in good health and they felt their medical insurance, in addition to Medicare, gave them ample coverage. They even had supplemental coverage just to be safe.

It was late in the fall of 1986 that Rose Sider's behavior started to change. Subtle changes were noted at first, then gradual changes of increasing magnitude to the degree where

MEDICAID AND LONG-TERM HEALTH CARE

Joe was having to devote most of his time to taking care of his wife. Unfortunately, by early spring of 1989 Joe was told by the doctor that it would be better for them both if Rose were to be entrusted to the care of a skilled nursing home facility since Rose had become too much to handle. All her needs had to be taken care of. She was rapidly becoming totally dependent on others, even for the most basic functions.

Sadly and painfully, Joe was forced to sit down with his eldest daughter, Sarah, who shared with her father the tremendous burden of rearranging her parents' lives to accommodate this tragedy that had befallen them. Both Sarah and Joe investigated every available possibility open to Joe regarding his wife. They all ended in the same sad bottom line—eventual impoverishment for Joe. Rose's expenses in a decent nursing home in Indiana in 1989 would run in the neighborhood of $25,000. This would mean that in a little more than three years Joe would go through their nest egg and then some. Finally, they came to the realization that their only hope was for Rose to go on Medicaid. Joe knew little about Medicaid. He had always been convinced that he had adequately provided for their later years and that Medicaid was a program only for indigents or welfare recipients.

What a tragic time this was for both Joe and his daughter, Sarah, as they set out to learn more about Medicaid and how Rose could qualify. First, they contacted their local Medicaid office. Speaking with a representative they learned the following: Anyone can qualify for Medicaid as long as their income and their assets are not in excess of the limits set by Medicaid. Initially, Joe did not even realize that even though Medicaid is a federal program, it is also a state program. Funding is matched equally from both sides and it is administered under the sovereignty of the individual state. The regulations vary from state to state, depending on the state's interpretation of the regulations.

Rose and Joe had their money in a jointly held savings account. The account required the signature of either Joe or Rose to withdraw money. Under Medicaid as administered by the State of Indiana, these funds are considered totally available to Rose, thus making her ineligible for Medicaid assistance until she "spends down" her assets to the acceptable Medicaid limit.

Joe also learned that his annual pension of $15,000 plus an additional $600 a month in Social Security would not only make him ineligible for the Medicaid program should he ever need to apply, but would presently put him in a position where Medicaid could ask him for money towards Rose's support in the nursing home.

Unfortunately, because Joe and Rose, like many senior couples in this country, were ignorant of the laws regarding Medicaid and how the individual states vary in their interpretation of those rules, Joe was to be left impoverished, except for his income which also would be evaluated by Medicaid. In Indiana, the state can deem some of the community spouse's income as eligible funds to go towards the support of the institutionalized spouse. This amount is to be determined by the state. All his hard earned savings were considered to be 100% accessible to Rose by Medicaid, thus literally wiping him out, three years after Rose was moved to a nursing home.

What Sarah and Joe didn't realize is that there were other options open to Joe which would have protected his savings:

(1) If Joe had known or had any suspicion that Rose would eventually need a nursing home, federal law allows a 30-month window for the transfer of assets and savings. Therefore, when Rose first started showing symptoms of change, Joe could have transferred all of Rose's assets into his name and preserved his savings.

(2) If Joe and Rose had moved to Florida as they had originally planned, Joe would have been allowed to take possession of their savings account, since in Florida a savings account with an "or" condition (either signature to withdraw funds) can be taken possession of by the community spouse. Florida is more liberal than Indiana in its interpretation of Medicaid regulations.

(3) Joe and Rose had the option with that same 30-month window of transferring their funds to their children and setting up a life estate, or possibly a certain type of trust fund, to protect their assets.

MEDICAID AND LONG-TERM HEALTH CARE

Of course, if this case were narrated in more detail there were probably more complex options that might have been available. In general, it is acceptable to say that Joe will suffer great financial loss because he did not know basic facts about Medicaid.

ANNE AND JACK FLEMING

A brief phone call at 1:05 a.m. on a Tuesday morning in early December changed Anne and Jack's life to a degree where things would never be quite the same.

Anne and Jack were both professionals living and practicing law in Washington, D.C. Jack worked as an attorney with the Justice Department, specializing in International Terrorism, and Anne was a junior partner with a firm specializing in litigation.

They had just spent the Thanksgiving holidays with Anne's parents in St. Louis. It had been a routine family gathering and there was ever-present the comfort that everybody was fine—especially Mother and Dad. Needless to say, Anne was totally unprepared when five days later she heard the frantic voice of her mother at the other end of the telephone with a cryptic message saying her father had suffered a major stroke and was lying in intensive care and when could she come out?

The following evening Anne found herself staring down at her father, whose vacant stare back left her totally numb. She suddenly realized that her mother seemed to be handling the situation better than she. However, painfully she recalled her discussion this afternoon with Dr. Bracken concerning her father's condition, concerning her mother and father as a couple facing the future, and specifically *her* role in all of this. It was with a crushing sinking feeling that seemed to overwhelm her that she realized that nothing in her life had prepared her for this—no schools, no classes, no courses, no friends, no prior life experience. This was all uncharted territory of which she had to try to make sense and yet she did not even have a clue as to how to begin.

The bad news was that the doctor had said that although her father would recover, he would never be independent again. From now on he would have to be looked after and taken care of for all his needs. Then there was her mother, as the doctor painfully reminded her, who at 74 was not a young woman. Her chronic arthritis and osteoporosis made her incapable of taking care of her husband and raised the question as to how long she would be capable of taking care of herself. This left the doctor with no choice but to strongly recommend a skilled nursing home facility for her father and perhaps for her mother too, in the not too distant future. How much longer did Anne feel she could rest easily knowing her mother's physical condition and knowing that she was living all alone in that big house!

All these questions and having to talk to her mother was making Anne physically ill in addition to exacerbating her already pounding headache.

Questions, questions, questions—they all seemed to fly out at her like three-dimensional objects off a movie screen.

Anne couldn't help but look back on many recent occasions when she and Jack had been at some sort of social function and inevitably, one person would eventually bring up the topic of long-term health care and all its ramifications. It seemed to be one of the hottest topics in Washington, at least recently. But somehow Anne always at that point would manage to excuse herself, either conveniently seeing someone she hadn't said hello to or definitely needing another glass of white wine. God, it was such an awful topic, almost like discussing death or cancer. Not only did she know nothing about the subject but she had no desire to learn anything, as she knew that long-term health care would almost surely never affect her directly. Her parents and Jack's parents were provided for, by owning their own homes, having ample savings accounts and generous health insurance coverage, including Medicare. As for herself and Jack, well, they were only in their late thirties and in relatively good health. Now all her rationales didn't seem to matter. How could she have been so very wrong . . . ? Now it was up to her to get all the answers. She knew that she alone would be responsible for providing for the future for her parents as they had once provided for hers. Anne felt a sense of agonizing responsibility.

MOTHER'S STORY

In spring 1987, my mother's behavior was not that of her normal self. She had been having difficulty remembering the names of simple everyday objects like a telephone or our car, for over a year. However, considering the fact that in July 1986 mother had spent over a month on the Neurological Floor at Columbia Presbyterian Medical Center, under the care of a highly respected New York psychiatrist who subsequently declared that she did not have Alzheimer's Disease, we thought nothing of it. Nevertheless, we could not ignore the fact that Mother was starting to object to Dad's leaving her by herself to go to the office. She simply could not stay alone. Dad engaged a companion to come and stay with Mother but even this arrangement did not satisfy her. Her anxiety continued. It was so frustrating not to be able to help her to feel comfortable or at least to be able to alleviate some of her suffering. Her facial expressions were most often anguished. Nothing seemed to alter this. Even her medication would either knock her out or was ineffective.

Eventually, in February 1987, it became necessary for me to temporarily move back in with my parents as Dad was no longer able to cope with the situation on his own. And, basically, I had to rely on commuting to Washington, one weekend a month, just to keep in touch with my life.

It was sometime in January 1987, prior to my moving in with my parents, that I began to realize the full impact of the drama that was unfolding in their lives and in mine. The once casual and veiled allusions to a nursing home for Mother, if she did not accept a companion or try to cope better, suddenly loomed as a grim but strong possibility. Dad was disintegrating before my eyes through frustration, depression, exhaustion and possibly worst of all, total incomprehension and disbelief at the magnitude of the events changing his life—their lives. Events over which he had no control.

As the situation in my parents' home continued to deteriorate, we had no choice but to once again turn to doctors and medicine for some answers. Subsequently, Mother was admitted to the Neurological/Psychiatric Floor at Mt. Sinai Medical Center in New York for more medical tests. After a period of two months, during which grueling and extensive tests were conducted on Mother, while Dad and I clung to the slim hope that whatever was plaguing her was remediable, the dreaded diagnosis was handed down to us—Alzheimer's. As definitively and as positively as can be diagnosed on a living person, Mother had Alzheimer's Disease. Even as I write this, I can still all too vividly recall that moment when the chilling, sinking feeling came over me at the sound of that word. I remember intently trying to listen to the doctor, even as my feelings grew stronger, while he continued to explain that Mother's condition would only worsen and went on to describe some of the symptoms we could expect to see develop over the next few years. Finally, he strongly recommended a skilled nursing home facility equipped to care for Alzheimer's patients, and then he wished us well.

The very word—nursing home—left me feeling numb. I had no idea of how one finds a nursing home—what is the cost of a nursing home—how one pays for a nursing home—or how to evaluate a nursing home. The whole subject of nursing homes was totally alien to me. I had never even thought about it for more than a fleeting moment, and then, not seriously. Now I not only had to think about it but deal with the sickening reality that this was for my mother and that she would probably be there for the rest of her life. That was a terrible realization which was emotionally overwhelming.

I had so wished that someone whom I trusted like myself, could have taken over at that point, and only when everything was resolved would I again assume responsibility. Unfortunately, that was not to be. Instead I had to go about finding answers to those questions and many more, knowing full well that the resulting decision that had to be made would shape the remainder of my parents' lives.

One of the most stressful aspects through all of this was the terrible sense of aloneness. It was as if no one could understand how I felt and I certainly could not have described it. It was almost as if I had become two people, one functioning in the capacity of a detached person who had to assume responsibility for this tragic project for this unfortunate family; the other a tremendously emotionally saddened daughter, watching helplessly as her parents' lives are shattered, their

MEDICAID AND LONG-TERM HEALTH CARE

dreams destroyed, their future now and forever separated, by one insidious word—Alzheimer's.

Looking back it seems Mother, even then, was sufficiently affected by the illness so as not to even fully realize the impact of her diagnosis. Her entire preoccupation was with maintaining her dignity and pride while struggling to appear nonplussed in the face of the doctor's continuing barrage of "senseless" questions. Mother could not understand why he was asking her the name of the President of the United States. Didn't he know? Anyway, she knew, she just couldn't recall it right now—and why did he want to know the day? It had to be Monday or Tuesday. And of course she knew what the object (a fork) was that he was holding up; she just couldn't think of the word. Mother then turned and looked plaintively toward Dad as if to say—please help me out. But the words never quite came. Indeed, she was never even quite able to sufficiently distract the doctor from focusing his attention on her progressive memory loss.

Fortunately, during most of this period I was able to detach myself enough to be able to do whatever was necessary to resolve the family crisis. There were calls to agencies, talking to professional counsellors, talking to hospital personnel and social workers, as well as writing to organizations, all in an effort to obtain some answers and information. The whole experience of trying to locate a good nursing home and obtain all the information necessary, seemed many times more difficult than it would have been ordinarily, due to being so emotionally stressed.

Information was never readily available. Some answers would only lead to more questions or some answers would lead to dead-ends. Phone calls were agonizingly frustrating, sometimes because of being transferred from one person to another and invariably ending up with the wrong person, and sometimes because of being put on hold interminably. Every day was a draining and exhausting one, with the situation never seeming any closer to resolution than the day before. In addition, there was for me the shock of learning that a skilled nursing home facility in New York City in 1987 would cost about $60,000 a year, or $5,000 a month. In my initial state of disbelief, I was sure that the monthly figure was actually the annual fee. How could any facility, where no one would voluntarily wish to become a resident, be so costly? And how would my family handle this expense over a period of years? The doctor had indicated that my mother could live with Alzheimer's anywhere from six to twenty years. Also, nursing home fees were exclusive of any medical expenses that might be incurred.

What further intensified the tremendous sadness that I tried to cope with was the realization that the resolution of this situation would only serve as a painful initiation into a life my parents would never have dreamt they would have to face.

In looking back, it is amazing that we actually live through situations that threaten to totally consume us. Somewhere, somehow, we find the strength, but certainly, I would have turned to a support group of some sort, had I been aware of its existence. Knowing that someone else has been through a similar experience or is presently going through one, is a tremendous source of strength.

Eventually, though, our situation was resolved on a more positive level. We found a very pleasant skilled nursing home facility in Florida, which currently provides the level of care Mother needs and affords her as much of life's comforts as she is capable of enjoying, and to date, there is no clear scientific method of determining how much a person in Mother's position can actually enjoy.

Fortunately, I had learned that it was not necessary for Mother to have prior residency in Florida to be accepted into a nursing home there. And once one becomes a permanent resident in the nursing home, Florida residency is immediate. I had also learned that Mother would be eligible for Medicaid as soon as her finances were exhausted or in Medicaid terminology "spent down." Considering the cost of the nursing home, conceivably that could be accomplished in a matter of months. But above all there was the reassurance that Mother would be more comfortable and generally do better all around in Florida because of the mild climate, pleasant physical surroundings and the high calibre of the nursing home staff—a reassurance that still gives me comfort.

Chapter 3

BASIC INFORMATION ON MEDICAID

(As Applied to Long-Term Health Care)

This chapter deals with some basic information and requirements for Medicaid in the Aged category which are generally applicable throughout all 50 states.

To apply for Medicaid a person must be *aged, reside* in the state in which he or she is applying, have the required legal status as a *citizen or legal alien,* and *be medically in need of* a nursing home facility, skilled or intermediate.

ELIGIBILITY REQUIREMENTS

(1) To qualify for the Medicaid category of "Aged," the age requirement is 65 or over.

(2) The residency requirement is usually immediate, meaning as soon as the person is in a long-term health care facility or nursing home he or she is considered a resident of that state, provided he or she also intends to stay in that state. *Durational residency is not a requirement.* (See Glossary.)

(3) The citizenship requirement is either United States citizenship or legal alien status. Some states are also working on including people who are eligible under the new Amnesty regulations. These people are referred to as LPRs or

LTRs—Legal Permanent Residents or Legal Temporary Residents.
(4) For long-term health care, the applicant must be medically in need of the level of care provided in a skilled nursing facility or intermediate care facility.
(5) For long-term health care, the applicant must find a nursing home with an available bed—willing to admit them.

INFORMATION ON INCOME AND RESOURCE CONSIDERATIONS

The Treatment of Spousal Income (Non-Medicaid Recipient)

Different states will treat the income of the community spouse—the one not in need of long-term health care—in various ways. There are some states in which the following rule applies:

Should the level of income of the community spouse be below a certain level (a figure which has been determined by the state in accordance with the Federal Poverty Level Income Guidelines), then the income of the institutionalized spouse can be deemed to the community spouse to raise his or her income level.

The following is an example of this situation:

Al is 78 and, having suffered a severe stroke, is being placed in a skilled nursing home facility where he will remain the rest of his life. Betty, his wife, is 73 and will remain in their home. Al's Social Security and retirement fund from the power company give him a combined income of about $990 a month. Betty's income is solely from Social Security and amounts to only $415 a month. The cost of the skilled nursing home is $3500 a month in his state, a figure Al can ill afford, but his financial circumstances make him eligible for Medicaid. As for Betty's income, since it is less than $815 per month, the minimum allowance for the community spouse, Al, by law, can divert $400 of his monthly income to Betty to bring her income up to the allowable $815 per month and Medicaid will pay the difference between Al's remaining income and the cost of the nursing home.

MEDICAID AND LONG-TERM HEALTH CARE

On the other hand, there are some states that require a contribution from the community spouse when financially feasible. These states are:

● Indiana, Nebraska, and West Virginia, which require contributions from the community spouse to reduce the amount of payment made by Medicaid. However, in West Virginia this applies only to the first six months after the spouse has entered into the nursing home facility. In Indiana and Nebraska, currently, it is an ongoing process.

● Colorado, Connecticut, Illinois, Minnesota, New Hampshire, New York, Rhode Island, Texas, Virginia, and Wisconsin require a contribution as calculated by a formula determined by that state. This contribution is expected to go towards mitigating the cost of the nursing home facility. In most of these states the courts are authorized to enforce this contribution, but in actuality such action is rarely, if ever, taken.

Considerations on Resources: Of Applicant and Spouse

Most states currently[1] follow the SSI guidelines in determining financial eligibility for a Medicaid applicant. These are the basic guidelines:

(A) Resources are defined as liquid or fixed—liquid assets are any assets which can be easily liquidated by the applicant: cash on hand, savings, checking accounts, stocks, bonds, mutual fund shares, promissory notes, etc. Fixed or non-liquid resources of the applicant generally are personal property, real property, automobiles and rental property.

(B) Resources owned solely by the community spouse are not counted when determining eligibility of the Medicaid applicant,

---

[1] The Catastrophic Health Bill changed this as of October 1989. See pages 23-24 (1, 2, 3 and 4).

beginning with the first full month after he or she has entered the nursing home facility.[2]

BASIC, OR "USUAL," EXEMPTIONS FROM COUNTABLE RESOURCES

Some basic assets which are excluded from countable resources and which are referred to in this book as the "usual exemptions" are:

(1) The homestead, if the community spouse or a dependent is residing there or if the applicant will be returning there.
(2) An automobile with up to $4,500 in market value. If the automobile is necessary for employment, medical needs, or has been modified in any way to accommodate a handicapped person, then its total market value is excluded. Nebraska and Hawaii, however, only exclude an automobile with market value of up to $1,500.[3]
(3) Life insurance is excluded up to $1,500 total face value on one individual in most states.
(4) Burial policy is also excluded up to $1,500 or higher if it is irrevocable.
(5) Property other than the homestead, such as real estate worth up to $6,000, is excluded in most states provided that it yields 6% or more in interest or income.
(6) Personal effects and household goods are also generally excluded if below $2,000 in value.[4]

The Medicaid recipient living in a long-term health care facility/nursing home is permitted a monthly allowance of between $30 and $60 for basic necessities.

---

[2]The Catastrophic Health Bill changed this as of October 1989. See pages 23-24 (1, 2, 3, and 4).

[3]See pages 23-24 (1, 2, 3, and 4).

[4]See pages 23-24 (1, 2, 3, and 4).

THE TRANSFER OF ASSETS FOR ELIGIBILITY REQUIREMENTS

To be considered eligible for Medicaid an applicant must transfer all assets at least 30 months (2 1/2 years) prior to submitting an application. However, some states still adhere to the old regulation of 24 months for the transfer of assets, but these are states which must introduce new legislation to be in compliance with the new regulation. The new regulation is the provision of the new Catastrophic Health Bill which took effect on July 1, 1988, relating to the transfer of assets for Medicaid eligibility. This section of the Medicare Catastrophic Health Bill is covered briefly in the next few pages.

There are a very few states where transfer of assets between spouses is not even a consideration since there are community property laws which treat all assets as just that—community property.

When assets are being transferred for the sake of Medicaid eligibility they cannot be transferred or liquidated for less than their full market value. For example, a second home appraised at $150,000 cannot be transferred to a son or daughter for $1,000.

THE MEDICARE CATASTROPHIC HEALTH BILL AS IT AFFECTS MEDICAID REGULATIONS[5]

The Medicare Catastrophic Coverage Act of 1988 was a very lengthy and extensive bill which was repealed on December 13, 1989. Only a small section of this bill affecting Medicaid for the Aged in a long-term health care facility is still in effect. This section was written specifically in an effort to protect the income and resources of the couples in order to guard against impoverishing the community spouse. Very briefly, it covers the following:

---

[5]Applying only to the spouses of individuals entering a nursing home facility after September 30, 1989.

SURVIVING THE NOT SO GOLDEN YEARS

(1) All states will be required to exempt the homestead from being included in countable resources provided the community spouse, or in some cases a dependent child, is living there. All personal property and household goods will be exempt.

(2) The transfer of assets for the purpose of meeting eligibility requirements for Medicaid must be completed 30 months prior to application. The previous time limit for such transfers was 24 months.

(3) Each state will determine the amount of liquid assets the community spouse is permitted to retain. This amount will range from a minimum of $12,516 to a maximum of $62,580, depending upon the state. In all states it will be one half of all assets providing that figure is not less than $12,516 and does not exceed $62,580. No resources of the community spouse will be considered available to the institutionalized spouse after he or she has been declared eligible for Medicaid.

(4) In applicable situations, the monthly income that can be retained by the community spouse will gradually be raised. Previously (prior to October 1, 1989), the Federal Poverty Income Level for a two-person family was $786 a month. During the period from October 1, 1989, to June 30, 1991, it will be increased to 122% of this level. From July 1, 1991, to June 30, 1992, the minimum is increased to 133% of this level. After July 1, 1992, the minimum is increased to 150% of this level, not to exceed a minimum of $1,500 per month.

GENERAL INFORMATION ON APPLYING FOR MEDICAID

When applying for Medicaid, the following general information is required (depending on the individual case and the state, more information may be necessary):

- birth certificate or other proof of age
- Social Security number (if you do not have one, you must apply for one to be eligible)
- any proof of earnings (if applicable)
- letters or forms with amount of income from Social Security, SSI, VA, pensions, etc.

MEDICAID AND LONG-TERM HEALTH CARE

- life insurance and medical insurance (forms or documents)
- savings books, bank statements, etc.
- information on ownership of real property and motor vehicles

It should be noted that the processing of all applications for Medicaid in all states usually takes between 30 and 45 days and in some states, 60 days. Also, when an applicant is approved by Medicaid, his or her status is reviewed annually. Any significant changes (such as an increase) in that person's financial standing could cause him or her to become ineligible for Medicaid.

Chapter 4

MEDICAID INFORMATION STATE BY STATE

BASIC ELIGIBILITY REQUIREMENTS, ADDRESSES, AND TELEPHONE NUMBERS

The following material is not intended to be a comparative or definitive analysis of the Medicaid regulations for the Aged Category. It is information intended to provide a state by state breakdown of the basic financial eligibility requirements for the Medicaid-Aged Category. The regulations may vary from state to state; therefore, the address and telephone number of each Medicaid office is listed for further individual information.

It should be noted that the rules covering the handling of the monthly income and the financial assets of the community spouse as given for each state on the following pages apply only to individuals who were permanent residents in nursing home facilities PRIOR *to October 1, 1989. See pages 23-24 (1, 2, 3, and 4).*

MEDICAID AND LONG-TERM HEALTH CARE

ALABAMA

The monthly income limit in determining eligibility for the Medicaid applicant/resident in a long-term health care facility/nursing home is $1,000, including all sources of income.

The monthly income of the community spouse is not considered by Medicaid when determining the eligibility of the institutionalized spouse 30 days after he or she has entered the private nursing home facility. However, during the first month, the combined income of both spouses is considered totally available to the Medicaid applicant.[1]

The financial assets limit in determining eligibility of the Medicaid applicant residing in a long-term health care facility/nursing home is $2,000 and the usual exemptions.

The financial assets of the community spouse are currently not considered by Medicaid in determining the eligibility of the institutionalized spouse, provided the community spouse has sole title to the asset.[2]

Joint assets are considered totally available to the Medicaid applicant unless this is rebutted by the community spouse. Any asset owned by the applicant is considered as a countable resource in determining eligibility.[3]

For further information or clarification as to the administration of the rules for Medicaid by the State of Alabama, write to:

Director
Alabama Medicaid Agency
2500 Fairlane Drive
Montgomery, AL 36130
Telephone: (205) 277-2710

---

[1]See page 23.

[2]See page 23.

[3]See page 23.

ALASKA

The monthly income limit in determining eligibility for the Medicaid applicant/resident in a long-term health care facility/nursing home is $1,158.

The monthly income of the community spouse is not considered by Medicaid when determining the eligibility of the institutionalized spouse.

The financial assets limit in determining eligibility of the Medicaid applicant residing in a long-term health care facility/nursing home is $2,000 and the usual exemptions.

The financial assets of the community spouse are currently not considered by Medicaid in determining the eligibility of the institutionalized spouse, six months after he or she enters the private nursing home facility, with efforts being made to change it to one month.[4]

Joint assets are considered totally available to each spouse. However, Alaska is one of two states that allows the transfer of resources by the recipient for the purposes of eligibility requirements, under special income standards.[5]

For further information or clarification as to the administration of the rules of Medicaid by the State of Alaska, write to:

Director
Division of Medical Assistance
Department of Health & Social Services
P.O. Box H-07
Juneau, AK 99811-0660
Telephone: (907) 465-3355

---

[4]See page 23.

[5]See page 23.

ARKANSAS

The monthly income limit in determining eligibility for the Medicaid applicant/resident in a long-term health care facility/nursing home is $1,158.

The monthly income of the community spouse is not considered by Medicaid when determining the eligibility of the institutionalized spouse.

The financial assets limit in determining eligibility of the Medicaid applicant residing in a long-term health care facility/nursing home is $2,000 and the usual exemptions.

The financial assets of the community spouse are currently not considered by Medicaid in determining the eligibility of the institutionalized spouse.[6]

Some assets are considered joint while others are not. Full value of jointly held assets is considered to be available to the applicant unless his or her ability to dispose of the asset is restricted. Assets held solely by the community spouse are considered unavailable to the applicant for Medicaid.[7]

For further information or clarification as to the interpretation of the regulations for Medicaid for the State of Arkansas, write to:

Director
Medical Eligibility Unit
P.O. Box 1437, Slot 1223
Little Rock, AR 72203
Telephone: (501) 682-8259,
    or toll-free (800) 482-5431

---

[6]See page 23.

[7]See page 23.

SURVIVING THE NOT SO GOLDEN YEARS

ARIZONA

The monthly income limit in determining eligibility for the Medicaid/AHCCCS applicant/resident in a long-term health care facility/nursing home is $1,158.

The monthly income of the community spouse is not considered by Medicaid/AHCCCS when determining the eligibility of the institutionalized spouse the next calendar month after he or she enters the private nursing home facility.

The financial assets limit in determining eligibility of the Medicaid/AHCCCS applicant residing in a long-term health care facility/nursing home is $2,000 and the usual exemptions.

The financial assets of the community spouse are currently not considered by Medicaid/AHCCCS in determining the eligibility of the institutionalized spouse, one to six months after he or she has entered the private nursing home facility.[8]

Joint assets are treated as belonging equally to each spouse.[9]

In Arizona, the state's equivalent of Medicaid is referred to as AHCCCS—Arizona Health Care Cost Containment System (the state health program for the needy).

For further information or clarification as to the administration of the rules for Medicaid/AHCCCS as administered by the State of Arizona, write to:

Director
Arizona Health Care Cost Containment System
Attention: Long-Term Care
P.O. Box 25520
Phoenix, AZ 85002
Telephone: (602) 234-3655,
   or toll-free (800) 654-8713

---

[8]See page 23.

[9]See page 23.

CALIFORNIA

In California, the State Medicaid program is referred to as Medi-Cal.

The monthly income limit in determining eligibility for the Medicaid/Medi-Cal applicant/resident in a long-term health care facility/nursing home is that it must be less than the monthly cost of the facility.

The monthly income of the community spouse is not considered by Medicaid/Medi-Cal when determining the eligibility of the institutionalized spouse. In California, two spouses can combine their income and divide it equally and the community spouse's share is left untouched by Medicaid/Medi-Cal.

In California, the financial assets of the community spouse, unless documented to be solely his or her property, are combined with those of the Medicaid/Medi-Cal applicant and then equally divided. The community spouse's share or assets are then not considered when determining the eligibility of the applicant for Medicaid/Medi-Cal.[10]

Joint assets in California are considered equally available to both parties; that is a 50/50 share. If this division is not accurate and if either spouse can produce a written agreement supporting that position, the state will then accept that agreement as legal, e.g., an agreement between spouses stating that a piece of real estate belongs solely to the community spouse because it has been in that person's family for 50 years.[11]

For further information or clarification as to the rules of Medicaid (Medi-Cal.) as administered by the State of California, write to:

Director
Medi-Cal. Program Inquiry Unit
State of California Health & Welfare Agency

---

[10] See page 23.

[11] See page 23.

Department of Health Services
714 P Street, Room 1692
Sacramento, CA 95814
Telephone: (916) 445-0266 or (916) 323-5861

COLORADO

The monthly income limit in determining eligibility for the Medicaid applicant/resident in a long-term health care facility/nursing home is $1,158.

The monthly income of the community spouse is not considered by Medicaid when determining the eligibility of the institutionalized spouse the next calendar month after he or she enters the private nursing home facility.

The financial assets limit in determining eligibility of the Medicaid applicant residing in a long-term health care facility/nursing home is $2,000 and the usual exemptions. The financial assets of the community spouse are currently not considered by Medicaid in determining the eligibility of the institutionalized spouse, the next calendar month after he or she enters the private nursing home facility.[12]

Jointly held assets are viewed as available to each spouse by percentage of ownership, except for joint bank accounts, which are considered totally available to the recipient.[13]

For further information or clarification as to the rules of Medicaid as administered by the State of Colorado, write to:

Director
Department of Social Services
1575 Sherman
P.O. Box 18100
Denver, CO 80203-1714
Telephone: (303) 866-3857 or (303) 866-3513

---

[12]See page 23.

[13]See page 23.

CONNECTICUT

The monthly income limit in determining eligibility for the Medicaid applicant/resident in a long-term health care facility/nursing home is that it must be less than the monthly cost of the facility.

The monthly income of the community spouse is not considered by Medicaid when determining the eligibility of the institutionalized spouse.

The financial assets limit in determining eligibility of the Medicaid applicant residing in a long-term health care facility/nursing home is $1,600 with the usual exemptions, except that in Connecticut burial funds are only excluded up to about $1,200.

The financial assets of the community spouse are currently not considered by Medicaid in determining the eligibility of the institutionalized spouse the next calendar month after he or she enters the private nursing home facility.[14]

Joint assets are considered to be totally available to the Medicaid applicant unless this can be rebutted by the community spouse and the resource can be determined to be held otherwise.[15]

For further information or clarification as to the rules of Medicaid as administered by the State of Connecticut, write to:

Director of Medicaid Policy
Department of Income Maintenance
State of Connecticut
110 Bartholomew Avenue
Hartford, CT 06106
Telephone: (203) 566-4019

---

[14]See page 23.

[15]See page 23.

DELAWARE

The monthly income limit in determining eligibility for the Medicaid applicant/resident in a long-term health care facility/nursing home is $792.40

The monthly income of the community spouse is not considered by Medicaid when determining the eligibility of the institutionalized spouse.

The financial assets limit in determining eligibility of the Medicaid applicant, residing in a long-term health care facility/nursing home is $2,000 and the usual exemptions.

The financial assets of the community spouse are currently not considered by Medicaid in determining the eligibility of the institutionalized spouse thirty days after he or she enters the private nursing home facility.[16]

Joint assets are viewed as equally available to both parties.[17]

For further information or clarification as to the rules of Medicaid as administered by the State of Delaware, write to:

Director
Department of Social Services
Robb Scott Building
Medicaid Long-Term Care
153 E. Chestnut Hill Road
Newark, DE 19713
Telephone: (302) 368-6610

DISTRICT OF COLUMBIA

The monthly income limit in determining eligibility for the Medicaid applicant/resident in a long-term health care facility/nursing home is that it must be less than the monthly cost of the facility.

---

[16]See page 23.

[17]See page 23.

The monthly income of the community spouse is not considered by Medicaid when determining the eligibility of the institutionalized spouse thirty days after he or she has entered the private nursing home facility.

The financial assets limit in determining eligibility of the Medicaid applicant residing in a long-term health care facility/nursing home is $2,700 and the usual exemptions.

The financial assets of the community spouse are currently not considered by Medicaid in determining the eligibility of the institutionalized spouse, after he or she enters the private nursing home facility.[18]

Joint assets are considered totally available to the applicant of Medicaid.[19]

For further information or clarification as to the rules of Medicaid as administered by the District of Columbia, write to:

Director (Medicaid Program Specialist)
Office of Policy & Planning
609 H Street, N.E.
5th Floor
Washington, DC 20002
Telephone: (202) 724-5168, (202) 724-5236, (202) 724-5173, or (202) 727-5951

FLORIDA

The monthly income limit in determining eligibility for the Medicaid applicant/resident in a long-term health care facility/nursing home is $1,158.

The monthly income of the community spouse is not considered by Medicaid when determining the eligibility of the institutionalized spouse.

---

[18]See page 23.

[19]See page 23.

SURVIVING THE NOT SO GOLDEN YEARS

The financial assets limit in determining eligibility of the Medicaid applicant residing in a long-term health care facility/nursing home is $2,000 and the usual exemptions.

The financial assets of the community spouse are currently not considered by Medicaid in determining the eligibility of the institutionalized spouse.[20]

Joint assets are treated differently. If the applicant is a joint account holder with unrestricted access to the funds in the account, these funds are then presumed to be totally available to him or her unless otherwise determined.[21]

For further information or clarification as to the administration of the rules of Medicaid by the State of Florida, write to:

Program Director
Aging and Adult Services
Department of Health & Rehabilitative Services
1317 Windwood Boulevard
Tallahassee, FL 32399-0700
Telephone: (904) 488-9235

GEORGIA

The monthly income limit in determining eligibility for the Medicaid applicant/resident in a long-term health care facility/nursing home is $1,158.

The monthly income of the community spouse is not considered by Medicaid when determining the eligibility of the institutionalized spouse the next calendar month after he or she enters the private nursing home facility.

The financial assets limit in determining eligibility of the Medicaid applicant residing in a long-term health care facility/nursing home is $2,000 and the usual exemptions.

The financial assets of the community spouse are currently not considered by Medicaid in determining the eligibility of the

---

[20]See page 23.

[21]See page 23.

institutionalized spouse thirty days after he or she enters the private nursing home facility.[22]

Joint assets are treated as such, but when an applicant has access to certain resources, these are then considered as countable resources towards Medicaid eligibility.[23]

For further information or clarification as to the administration of the rules of Medicaid by the State of Georgia, write to:

Director
Medicaid Program
State of Georgia
Department of Medical Assistance
Floyd Veterans Memorial Building, West Tower
Suite 1204
2 Martin Luther King, Jr. Drive, S.E.
Atlanta, GA 30334
Telephone: (404) 656-4347

HAWAII

The monthly income limit in determining eligibility for the Medicaid applicant/resident in a long-term health care facility/nursing home is that it must be less than the monthly cost of the facility.

The monthly income of the community spouse is not considered by Medicaid when determining the eligibility of the institutionalized spouse thirty days after he or she has entered the private nursing home facility.

The financial assets limit in determining eligibility of the Medicaid applicant residing in a long-term health care facility/nursing home is $2,000 and the usual exemptions.

The financial assets of the community spouse are currently not considered by Medicaid in determining the eligibility of the

---

[22]See page 23.

[23]See page 23.

institutionalized spouse thirty days after he or she enters the private nursing home facility.[24]

Joint assets are only considered as such, if both names are on the resources, and then they are considered to be totally available to the recipient. This can be rebutted by the community spouse.[25]

For further information or clarification as to the rules of Medicaid as administered by the State of Hawaii, write to:

Director
Health Care Administration Division
P.O. Box 339
Honolulu, HI 96809-0339
Telephone: (808) 548-3855

IDAHO

The monthly income limit in determining eligibility for the Medicaid applicant/resident in a long-term health care facility/nursing home is $1,158.

The monthly income of the community spouse is not considered by Medicaid when determining the eligibility of the institutionalized spouse.

The financial assets limit in determining eligibility of the Medicaid applicant residing in a long-term health care facility/nursing home is $2,000 and the usual exemptions.

The financial assets of the community spouse are currently not considered by Medicaid in determining the eligibility of the institutionalized spouse the next calendar month after he or she enters the private nursing home facility.[26]

---

[24]See page 23.

[25]See page 23.

[26]See page 23.

Joint assets are considered in determining eligibility for Medicaid, according to their availability to the applicant.[27]

For further information or clarification as to the rules of Medicaid as administered by the State of Idaho, write to:

Director
Bureau of Welfare Programs
Department of Health and Welfare
Boise, ID 83720-9990
Telephone: (208) 334-5819

ILLINOIS

The monthly income limit in determining eligibility for the Medicaid applicant/resident in a long-term health care facility/nursing home is that it must be less than the monthly cost of the facility.

The monthly income of the community spouse is determined by the Illinois Department of Public Aid's Code and Responsible Relative Support Policy. If their income exceeds this limit, then legal action can be taken to force the community spouse to contribute toward the income of the spouse residing in the nursing home, including the cost of the facility.[28]

The financial assets limit in determining eligibility of the Medicaid applicant residing in a long-term health care facility/nursing home is $2,000 and the usual exemptions.

The financial assets of the community spouse are currently not considered by Medicaid in determining the eligibility of the institutionalized spouse.[29]

---

[27]See page 23.

[28]See page 23.

[29]See page 23.

Joint assets are viewed as totally accessible to the applicant, except in certain instances.[30]

For further information or clarification as to the rules of Medicaid as administered by the State of Illinois, write to:

Director
Bureau of Policies and Procedure
Illinois Department of Public Aid
Jesse B. Harris Building
100 S. Grand Avenue East
Springfield, IL 62762
Telephone: (217) 782-1239
Responsible Relative Unit: (217) 785-9729

INDIANA

The monthly income limit in determining eligibility for the Medicaid applicant/resident in a long-term health care facility/nursing home is that it must be less than the monthly cost of the facility.

The maximum monthly income for the community spouse is $710.68 net. Any sum in excess of this can be deemed to the institutional spouse, in which case the community spouse can demonstrate to the agency by way of rebuttal—documents such as bills—substantiating his need for more financial resources to cover his monthly living expenses.[31]

The financial assets limit, in determining eligibility for the applicant of Medicaid residing in a long-term health care facility/nursing home is $1,500 and the usual exemptions.

The financial assets limit for the community spouse in determining eligibility of the institutionalized spouse is $2,250.[32]

Burial Contract, in Indiana, is exempt, only if irrevocable.

---

[30]See page 23.

[31]See page 23.

[32]See page 23.

MEDICAID AND LONG-TERM HEALTH CARE

Life insurance in Indiana is exempt only if all life insurance policies on their face, in total, do not exceed $1,400 and provided the beneficiary is the state or funeral home.

Joint assets in Indiana are always viewed as totally available to the Medicaid recipient.[33]

For further information or clarification as to the rules of Medicaid as administered by the State of Indiana, write to:

Director
Department of Public Welfare
100 North Senate Avenue, Room 701
Indianapolis, IN 46204
Telephone: (317) 232-4966

IOWA

The monthly income limit in determining eligibility for the Medicaid applicant/resident in a long-term health care facility/nursing home is $1,158.

The monthly income of the community spouse is not considered by Medicaid when determining the eligibility of the institutionalized spouse.

The financial assets limit in determining eligibility of the Medicaid applicant residing in a long-term health care facility/nursing home is $2,000 and the usual exemptions.

The financial assets of the community spouse are currently not considered by Medicaid in determining the eligibility of the institutionalized spouse.[34]

Jointly owned assets, if liquid, are considered totally available to the recipient of Medicaid. If they are titled, they are considered as specified on the title.[35]

---

[33]See page 23.

[34]See page 23.

[35]See page 23.

For further information or clarification as to the rules governing Medicaid as administered by the State of Iowa, write to:

    Director
    Department of Human Services
    Division of Medical Services
    Hoover State Office Building, 5th Floor
    Des Moines, IA 50219-0114
    Telephone: (515) 281-8621 or (515) 281-5586

KANSAS

The monthly income limit in determining eligibility for the Medicaid applicant/resident in a long-term health care facility/nursing home is that it must be less than the monthly cost of the facility.

The monthly income of the community spouse is not considered by Medicaid when determining the eligibility of the institutionalized spouse.

The financial assets limit in determining eligibility of the Medicaid applicant residing in a long-term health care facility/nursing home is $2,000 and the usual exemptions.

The financial assets of the community spouse are currently not considered by Medicaid in determining the eligibility of the institutionalized spouse the next calendar month after he or she enters the private nursing home facility.[36]

Joint resources are considered to be equally owned by both unless proven otherwise.[37]

For further information or clarification as to the rules of Medicaid as administered by the State of Kansas, write to:

    Constituent Liaison
    I.M. Policy Section

---

[36]See page 23.

[37]See page 23.

MEDICAID AND LONG-TERM HEALTH CARE

State of Kansas
State Department of Social & Rehabilitation Services
Docking State Office Building
Room 624 South
Topeka, KS 66612-1570
Telephone: (913) 296-3349

KENTUCKY

The monthly income limit in determining eligibility for the Medicaid applicant/resident in a long-term health care facility/nursing home is $1,158.

The monthly income of the community spouse is not considered by Medicaid when determining the eligibility of the institutionalized spouse.

The financial assets limit in determining eligibility of the Medicaid applicant residing in a long-term health care facility/nursing home is $2,000 and the usual exemptions.

The financial assets of the community spouse are currently not considered by Medicaid in determining the eligibility of the institutionalized spouse, one month after their separation has occurred.[38]

Joint assets are considered totally available to the recipient if he/she has legal access to the asset.[39]

For further information or clarification as to the rules of Medicaid as administered by the State of Kentucky, write to:

Director
Department of Eligibility Services
275 E. Main Street
6th Floor
Frankfort, KY 40621
Telephone: (502) 564-7050

---

[38]See page 23.

[39]See page 23.

LOUISIANA

The monthly income limit in determining eligibility for the Medicaid applicant/resident in a long-term health care facility/nursing home is $1,158.

The monthly income of the community spouse is not considered by Medicaid when determining the eligibility of the institutionalized spouse thirty days after he or she has entered the private nursing home facility.

For the first month the two incomes are combined and $186.80 is subtracted from the total and if the remainder is in excess of $1,158, then the applicant is considered ineligible.[40]

The financial assets limit in determining eligibility of the Medicaid applicant residing in a long-term health care facility/nursing home is $2,000 and the usual exemptions.

The financial assets of the community spouse are currently not considered by Medicaid in determining the eligibility of the institutionalized spouse thirty days after he or she enters the private nursing home facility. For the first month the resources are combined and cannot exceed $3,000 for eligibility of the applicant.[41]

Joint assets are considered totally accessible to the Medicaid recipient and cannot exceed the $3,000 couple limit. However, the community spouse can take over ownership of any joint asset when power of attorney is not required to exercise this right.[42]

For further information or clarification as to the rules of Medicaid as administered by the State of Louisiana, write to:

Director
Medical Assistance Program
State of Louisiana
Department of Health & Hospitals
755 Riverside North

---

[40]See page 23.

[41]See page 23.

[42]See page 23.

MEDICAID AND LONG-TERM HEALTH CARE

P.O. Box 94065
Baton Rouge, LA 60804-4065
Telephone: (504) 342-3956

MAINE

The monthly income limit in determining eligibility for the Medicaid applicant/resident in a long-term health care facility/nursing home is that it must be less than the monthly cost of the facility.

The monthly income of the community spouse is not considered by Medicaid when determining the eligibility of the institutionalized spouse.

The financial assets limit in determining eligibility of the Medicaid applicant residing in a long-term health care facility/nursing home is $2,000 and the usual exemptions.

The financial assets of the community spouse are currently not considered by Medicaid in determining the eligibility of the institutionalized spouse.[43]

Jointly held assets or property are viewed by Medicaid as totally accessible to the applicant. The community spouse has a right to demonstrate how much of these assets he or she contributed to, and then remove that portion so that it would no longer be considered available to the Medicaid recipient.[44]

For further information or clarification regarding the administering of Medicaid in the State of Maine, write to the following:

Medicaid Program Manager
State House Station II
Bureau of Income Maintenance
Whitten Road
Augusta, ME 04333
Telephone: (207) 289-5098

---

[43]See page 23.

[44]See page 23.

MARYLAND

The monthly income limit in determining eligibility for the Medicaid applicant/resident in a long-term health care facility/nursing home is that it must be less than the monthly cost of the facility.

The monthly income of the community spouse is not considered by Medicaid when determining the eligibility of the institutionalized spouse the next calendar month after he or she enters the private nursing home facility.

The financial assets limit in determining eligibility of the Medicaid applicant residing in a long-term health care facility/nursing home is $2,500 and the usual exemptions.

The community spouse can only retain one-half of any financial asset, regardless of whether it is in his/her name or joint.[45]

Joint assets or single assets are considered equally accessible to both spouses and the applicant of Medicaid must spend down his or her share, to meet eligibility requirements.[46]

For further information or clarification as to the rules of Medicaid as administered by the State of Maryland, write to:

Director
Health Systems Financing Administration
Department of Health and Mental Hygiene
300 West Preston Street
Baltimore, MD 21201
Telephone: (301) 361-2018

MASSACHUSETTS

The monthly income limit in determining eligibility for the Medicaid applicant/resident in a long-term health care facili-

---

[45]See page 23.

[46]See page 23.

ty/nursing home is that it must be less than the monthly cost of the facility.

The monthly income of the community spouse is not considered by Medicaid when determining the eligibility of the institutionalized spouse.

The financial assets limit for the recipient of Medicaid is $2,000 plus a separate burial and identification account of $2,500. Neither this original account nor its interest can be touched; otherwise it becomes fully countable.

The financial assets of the community spouse are currently not considered by Medicaid in determining the eligibility of the institutionalized spouse, thirty days after he or she enters the private nursing home facility.[47]

Joint bank accounts are considered to be available in full to either party. In the case of all other assets, equal distribution is presumed unless otherwise demonstrated.[48]

For further information or clarification as to the rules of Medicaid as administered by the State of Massachusetts, write to:

Director
Department of Public Welfare
Eligibility Operations
Medicaid Division
180 Tremont Street
Boston, MA 02111
Telephone: (617) 574-0439 or (617) 348-5570

MICHIGAN

The monthly income limit in determining eligibility for the Medicaid applicant/resident in a long-term health care facility/nursing home is that it must be less than the monthly cost of the facility.

---

[47]See page 23.

[48]See page 23.

The monthly income of the community spouse is not considered by Medicaid when determining the eligibility of the institutionalized spouse.

The financial assets limit in determining eligibility of the Medicaid applicant residing in a long-term health care facility/nursing home is $2,000 and the usual exemptions.

The following joint assets are considered equally accessible to both spouses, meaning 50% available:[49]

- saving account
- checking account
- credit union share accounts
- credit union draft accounts
- certificates of deposit
- U.S. Savings Bonds
- individual retirement accounts (I.R.A.)
- Keogh plans
- nursing home patient trust funds
- prepaid funeral contracts

The following assets are not counted jointly:[50]

- your home in Michigan
- personal belongings
- one car
- burial plot for community spouse and applicant
- income-producing real estate. The annual income after expenses must equal at least about 6% of your equity.
- irrevocable prepaid funeral contracts
- first $1,000 cash surrender value of life insurance
- all your life insurance if you are at least age 70 or terminally ill
- assets that the recipient of Medicaid does not have the legal right to sell or use
- assets that the recipient has been unable to sell

---

[49]See page 23.

[50]See page 23.

For further information or clarification regarding the interpretation of the regulations for Medicaid in the State of Michigan, write to:

Director
Field Policy in Operations Administration
Department of Social Services
300 South Capitol Avenue
P.O. Box 30037
Lansing, MI 48909
Telephone: (517) 335-2737

MINNESOTA

The monthly income limit in determining eligibility for the Medicaid applicant/resident in a long-term health care facility/nursing home is that it must be less than the monthly cost of the facility.

The monthly income of the community spouse is not considered by Medicaid when determining the eligibility of the institutionalized spouse.

The financial assets limit in determining eligibility of the Medicaid applicant residing in a long-term health care facility/nursing home is $3,000 and the usual exemptions.

The financial assets of the community spouse are currently not considered by Medicaid in determining the eligibility of the institutionalized spouse.[51]

Joint assets are split equally unless a different ownership can be demonstrated beyond a reasonable doubt.[52]

For further information or clarification as to the rules of Medicaid as administered by the State of Minnesota, write to:

Director
Health Care Management

---

[51]See page 23.

[52]See page 23.

SURVIVING THE NOT SO GOLDEN YEARS

State of Minnesota
Department of Human Services
444 Lafayette Road
St. Paul, MN 55155
Attention: Long-Term Care
Telephone: (612) 296-6117, (612) 296-2738, or (612) 296-8517

MISSISSIPPI

The monthly income limit in determining eligibility for the Medicaid applicant/resident in a long-term health care facility/nursing home is $1,158.

The monthly income of the community spouse is not considered by Medicaid when determining the eligibility of the institutionalized spouse.

The financial assets limit in determining eligibility of the Medicaid applicant residing in a long-term health care facility/nursing home is $2,000 and the usual exemptions.

The financial assets of the community spouse are currently not considered by Medicaid in determining the eligibility of the institutionalized spouse.[53]

Joint assets are considered by Medicaid to be fully available to the recipient if the recipient's name is on the asset.[54]

For further information or clarification as to the rules of Medicaid as administered by the State of Mississippi, write to the following:

Director
Office of the Governor
Division of Medicaid
239 North Lamar Street
P.O. Box 2
801 Robert E. Lee Building

---

[53]See page 23.

[54]See page 23.

Jackson, MS 39201-1311
Telephone: (601) 359-6050

MISSOURI

The monthly income limit in determining eligibility for the Medicaid applicant/resident in a long-term health care facility/nursing home is that it must be less than the monthly cost of the facility.

The monthly income of the community spouse is not considered by Medicaid when determining the eligibility of the institutionalized spouse.

The financial assets limit in determining eligibility of the Medicaid applicant residing in a long-term health care facility/nursing home is $999 and the usual exemptions.

In the case of an application for Medicaid the spouse and the applicants total resources cannot exceed approximately $27,000—this is including the homestead. Resources include cash and securities in personal possession, ones in a safety deposit box, deposits in banks, postal savings, buildings and loan or trust companies, stocks, bonds, mortgages, promissory notes, savings bonds, building and loan certificates, personal notes, bills of exchange, bank checks, certificates of deposit, and similar instruments, both negotiable and non-negotiable. Personal property and cash-surrender value of life insurance will also be considered as a resource if the claimant can and should use it in meeting his/her needs.[55]

In Missouri, a husband and wife are considered as one, when computing the resources and/or property factors.[56]

For further information or clarification as to the rules governing Medicaid as administered by the State of Missouri, write to:

---

[55]See page 23.

[56]See page 23.

SURVIVING THE NOT SO GOLDEN YEARS

Director
Department of Social Services
Division of Family Services
P.O. Box 88
Jefferson City, MO 65103
Telephone: (314) 751-3425

MONTANA

The monthly income limit in determining eligibility for the Medicaid applicant/resident in a long-term health care facility/nursing home is that it must be less than the monthly cost of the facility.

The monthly income of the community spouse is not considered by Medicaid when determining the eligibility of the institutionalized spouse.

The financial assets limit in determining eligibility of the Medicaid applicant residing in a long-term health care facility/nursing home is $2,000 and the usual exemptions.

The financial assets of the community spouse are currently not considered by Medicaid in determining the eligibility of the institutionalized spouse thirty days after he or she enters the private nursing home facility.[57]

Joint resources are considered totally available to each spouse, therefore the applicant is presumed to own 100% of the assets, unless otherwise demonstrated.[58]

For further information or clarification as to the rules of Medicaid as administered by the State of Montana, write to:

Director
Medicaid Services New Division
Department of Social & Rehabilitative Services
P.O. Box 4210

---

[57]See page 23.

[58]See page 23.

Helena, MT 59604
Telephone: (406) 444-4540

NEBRASKA

The monthly income limit in determining eligibility for the Medicaid applicant/resident in a long-term health care facility/nursing home is that it must be less than the monthly cost of the facility.

The monthly income limit of the community spouse when determining the eligibility of the institutionalized spouse for Medicaid is $475 per month.

The financial assets limit in determining eligibility of the Medicaid applicant residing in a long-term health care facility/nursing home is $2,000 and the usual exemptions.

The financial assets for the community spouse are currently considered by Medicaid in determining the eligibility of the institutionalized spouse and cannot exceed $25,000.[59]

Joint assets are considered when determining eligibility and viewed as equally available to both.[60]

For further information or clarification regarding the interpretation of the regulations on Medicaid in the State of Nebraska, write to:

Director
Public Assistance Unit
Department of Social Services
P.O. Box 9506
Lincoln, NE 60509-5026
Telephone: (402) 471-9267

---

[59]See page 23.

[60]See page 23.

NEVADA

The monthly income limit in determining eligibility for the Medicaid applicant/resident in a long-term health care facility/nursing home is $714.

The monthly income of the community spouse is not considered by Medicaid when determining the eligibility of the institutionalized spouse.

The financial assets limit in determining eligibility of the Medicaid applicant residing in a long-term health care facility/nursing home is $2,000 and the usual exemptions.

The financial assets of the community spouse are currently not considered by Medicaid in determining the eligibility of the institutionalized spouse seven months after he or she enters the private nursing home facility.[61]

Joint property is assessed for resource accountability; only the legal share of the applicant for Medicaid is evaluated.[62]

For further information or clarification as to the rules of Medicaid as administered by the State of Nevada, write to:

Director
Eligibility and Payments
Department of Human Resources
Welfare Division
2527 North Carson Street
Carson City, NV 89710
Telephone: (702) 687-4976 or (702) 687-5765

NEW HAMPSHIRE

The monthly income limit in determining eligibility for the Medicaid applicant/resident in a long-term health care facility/nursing home is that it must be less than the monthly cost of the facility.

---

[61]See page 23.

[62]See page 23.

MEDICAID AND LONG-TERM HEALTH CARE

The monthly income of the community spouse is not considered by Medicaid when determining the eligibility of the institutionalized spouse.

The financial assets limit in determining eligibility of the Medicaid applicant residing in a long-term health care facility/nursing home is $2,500 and the usual exemptions.

The financial assets of the community spouse are currently not considered by Medicaid in determining the eligibility of the institutionalized spouse.[63]

Joint assets are divided equally between both spouses.[64]

For further information or clarification as to the rules of Medicaid as administered by the State of New Hampshire, write to:

Director
Office of Economic Services
State of New Hampshire
Department of Health & Human Services
Division of Human Services
6 Hazen Drive
Concord, NH 03301-6521
Telephone: (603) 271-4238
 or toll-free (800) 852-3345

NEW JERSEY

The monthly income limit in determining eligibility for the Medicaid applicant/resident in a long-term health care facility/nursing home is $1,158.

The monthly income of the community spouse is not considered by Medicaid when determining the eligibility of the institutionalized spouse.

---

[63]See page 23.

[64]See page 23.

The financial assets limit in determining eligibility of the Medicaid applicant residing in a long-term health care facility/nursing home is $2,000 and the usual exemptions.

The financial assets of the community spouse are currently not considered by Medicaid in determining the eligibility of the institutionalized spouse.[65]

Joint resources are treated as if totally available to the recipient if they are available to both equally—e.g., an "or" bank account is looked upon as totally available to the recipient.[66]

For further information or clarification as to the rules of Medicaid as administered by the State of New Jersey, write to:

Director
Division of Medical Assistance and Health Services
Department of Human Services
CN712
Trenton, NJ 08625
Telephone: (609) 588-2556

NEW MEXICO

The monthly income limit in determining eligibility for the Medicaid applicant/resident in a long-term health care facility/nursing home is $1,158.

The monthly income of the community spouse is combined with the monthly income of the applicant and divided in half to determine eligibility for Medicaid.

The financial assets limit in determining eligibility of the Medicaid applicant residing in a long-term health care facility/nursing home is $2,000 and the usual exemptions.

The financial assets of the community spouse are considered to be joint, with the exception of $30,000, which can be transferred exclusively to the community spouse if necessary

---

[65]See page 23.

[66]See page 23.

and retained by the community spouse as his/her exclusive asset.[67]

Joint assets are considered to be one-half the applicant's, unless they can be determined as exclusively belonging to the community spouse, because they were earned prior to the marriage, or because they are an inheritance, or any other fact which would qualify them as exclusively belonging to the community spouse.[68]

For further information or clarification as to the rules of Medicaid as administered by the State of New Mexico, write to:

Director
Human Services Department
Medical Assistance Division
P.O. Box 2348
Santa Fe, NM 87504-2348
Telephone: (505) 827-4315 or (505) 827-4319

NEW YORK

The monthly income limit in determining eligibility for the Medicaid applicant/resident in a long-term health care facility/nursing home is that it must be less than the monthly cost of the facility.

The monthly income of the community spouse is not considered by Medicaid when determining the eligibility of the institutionalized spouse.

The financial assets limit in determining eligibility of the Medicaid applicant residing in a long-term health care facility/nursing home is $3,250 and the usual exemptions.

The financial assets of the community spouse are currently not considered by Medicaid in determining the eligibility of the institutionalized spouse. However, in New York, it is at the discretion of the county whether to take legal action in order to

---

[67]See page 23.

[68]See page 23.

force a spouse to contribute towards the support of the institutionalized spouse.[69]

Joint assets are generally assumed to be evenly divided. If the claim is otherwise, documentation must be provided to substantiate this claim.[70]

For further information or clarification as to the rules of Medicaid as administered by the State of New York, write to:

>Director, Bureau of Long Term Care
>Eligibility Policy
>Division of Medical Assistance
>Department of Social Services
>40 North Pearl Street
>Albany, NY 12243-0001
>Telephone: (518) 473-5611

NORTH CAROLINA

The monthly income limit in determining eligibility for the Medicaid applicant/resident in a long-term health care facility/nursing home is that it must be less than the monthly cost of the facility.

The monthly income of the community spouse is not considered by Medicaid when determining the eligibility of the institutionalized spouse the next calendar month after he or she enters the private nursing home facility.

The financial assets limit in determining eligibility of the Medicaid applicant residing in a long-term health care facility/nursing home is $1,500 and the usual exemptions.

The financial assets of the community spouse are currently not considered by Medicaid in determining the eligibility of the institutionalized spouse the next calendar month after he or she enters the private nursing home facility.[71]

---

[69] See page 23.

[70] See page 23.

[71] See page 23.

MEDICAID AND LONG-TERM HEALTH CARE

Jointly held assets that can be disposed of without the consent of the other spouse are considered totally available to the Medicaid recipient.[72]

For further information or clarification as to the rules of Medicaid as administered by the State of North Carolina, write to:

Director
Division of Medical Assistance
Medicaid Eligibility Section
1985 Umstead Drive
Raleigh, NC 27603
Attention: Long-Term Care
Telephone: (919) 733-4600

NORTH DAKOTA

The monthly income limit in determining eligibility for the Medicaid applicant/resident in a long-term health care facility/nursing home is that it must be less than the monthly cost of the facility.

The monthly income limit for the community spouse when determining the eligibility of the institutionalized spouse for Medicaid is $345 a month.[73]

The financial assets limit in determining eligibility of the Medicaid applicant residing in a long-term health care facility/nursing home is $3,000 in real property and liquid assets and $3,000 in pre-need burial contract.

The financial assets limit for the community spouse, currently considered by Medicaid in determining the eligibility of the institutionalized spouse, is the same as for the applicant plus an additional $25,000.[74]

---

[72]See page 23.

[73]See page 23.

[74]See page 23.

Joint assets are divided in half with equal amounts available to each spouse.[75]

For further information or clarification as to the interpretation of the regulations on Medicaid by the State of North Dakota, write to:

Director of Medical Services
North Dakota Department of Human Services
State Capitol
600 E. Boulevard Avenue
Bismarck, ND 58505
Telephone: (701) 224-2321

OHIO

The monthly income limit in determining eligibility for the Medicaid applicant/resident in a long-term health care facility/nursing home is $1,158.

The monthly income of the community spouse is not considered by Medicaid when determining the eligibility of the institutionalized spouse the next calendar month after he or she enters the private nursing home facility.

The financial assets limit in determining eligibility of the Medicaid applicant residing in a long-term health care facility/nursing home is $1,500 and the usual exemptions.

The financial assets of the community spouse are currently not considered by Medicaid in determining the eligibility of the institutionalized spouse the next calendar month after he or she enters the private nursing home facility.[76]

Joint assets are evaluated for each individual's contribution, share, and access to the resource. Only the resources credited to the applicant/recipient are counted toward the applicable resource limitation. However, during the first month of separation from the community spouse, the applicant/reci-

---

[75]See page 23.

[76]See page 23.

pient and the community spouse's assets/resources are combined and applied toward the couple's resource limit. The month after the applicant/recipient has been institutionalized, he/she is considered an individual and as such his/her assets above are compared to the individual resource limit.[77]

For further information or clarification as to the rules of Medicaid as administered by the State of Ohio, write to:

    Director of Medicaid
    Bureau of Public Assistance Policy
    Ohio Department of Human Services
    30 East Broad Street, 27th Floor
    Columbus, OH 43266-0423
    Telephone: (614) 466-6024 or (614) 752-9701
    The toll-free (in-state) number for any disputes as to eligibility is (800) 282-1190

OKLAHOMA

The monthly income limit in determining eligibility for the Medicaid applicant/resident in a long-term health care facility/nursing home is $1,158.

The monthly income of the community spouse is not considered by Medicaid when determining the eligibility of the institutionalized spouse the next calendar month after he or she enters the private nursing home facility.

The financial assets limit in determining eligibility of the Medicaid applicant residing in a long-term health care facility/nursing home is $2,000 and the usual exemptions.

The financial assets of the community spouse are currently not considered by Medicaid in determining the eligibility of the institutionalized spouse, thirty days after he or she enters the private nursing home facility.[78]

---

[77] See page 23.

[78] See page 23.

SURVIVING THE NOT SO GOLDEN YEARS

Joint assets are divided equally between the community spouse and the spouse in the nursing home/long-term health care facility.[79]

For further information or clarification as to the rules of Medicaid as administered by the State of Oklahoma, write to:

Director
Department of Human Services
Medical Services Division
Long-Term Care
Lincoln Plaza Office Center
P.O. Box 25352
Oklahoma City, OK 73125
Telephone: (405) 557-2539

OREGON

The monthly income limit in determining eligibility for the Medicaid applicant/resident in a long-term health care facility/nursing home is $1,158, or if monthly income is higher, the applicant may qualify as "medically needy."

The monthly income of the community spouse is not considered by Medicaid when determining the eligibility of the institutionalized spouse thirty days after he or she has entered the private nursing home facility.

The financial assets limit in determining eligibility of the Medicaid applicant residing in a long-term health care facility/nursing home is $2,000 and the usual exemptions.

The financial assets of the community spouse are currently not considered by Medicaid in determining the eligibility of the institutionalized spouse.[80]

Assets are judged as liquid or fixed using the same criteria as the Federal SSI Program.[81]

---

[79]See page 23.

[80]See page 23.

[81]See page 23.

MEDICAID AND LONG-TERM HEALTH CARE

Jointly held assets are considered entirely available to the recipient. If there is a legal barrier towards disposing of these resources, then they may be retained by the community spouse.[82]

For further information or clarification as to the rules of Medicaid in the State of Oregon, write to:

Director
Department of Human Resources
Senior Services Division
313 Public Service Building
Salem, OR 97310
Telephone: (503) 378-3751

PENNSYLVANIA

The monthly income limit in determining eligibility for the Medicaid applicant/resident in a long-term health care facility/nursing home is that it must be less than the monthly cost of the facility.

The monthly income of the community spouse is not considered by Medicaid when determining the eligibility of the institutionalized spouse the next calendar month after he or she enters the private nursing home facility.

The financial assets limit in determining eligibility of the Medicaid applicant residing in a long-term health care facility/nursing home is $2,400 and the usual exemptions.

The financial assets of the community spouse are currently not considered by Medicaid in determining the eligibility of the institutionalized spouse the next calendar month after he or she enters the private nursing home facility.[83]

Joint assets are considered to be equally accessible to each spouse. However if one of the owners cannot sell without the

---

[82]See page 23.

[83]See page 23.

consent of the other and that consent is withheld, the resource is then considered unavailable.[84]

For further information or clarification as to the administration of Medicaid regulations by the State of Pennsylvania, write to:

>Director
>Bureau of Policy
>Division of Medical Assistance Eligibility
>Department of Public Welfare
>Willow Oak Building #42
>P.O. Box 2675
>Room 230
>Harrisburg, PA 17112
>Telephone: (717) 257-7815

RHODE ISLAND

The monthly income limit in determining eligibility for the Medicaid applicant/resident in a long-term health care facility/nursing home is that it must be less than the monthly cost of the facility.

The monthly income of the community spouse is not considered by Medicaid when determining the eligibility of the institutionalized spouse.

The financial assets limit in determining eligibility of the Medicaid applicant residing in a long-term health care facility/nursing home is $4,000 in liquid resources, $4,000 in real estate, the face value of life insurance and $5,000 in personal property (jewelry, etc.).

The financial assets of the community spouse are currently not considered by Medicaid in determining the eligibility of the institutionalized spouse, in most cases one month after he or

---

[84]See page 23.

she enters the private nursing home facility, and in all cases not after six months.[85]

Joint resources will be treated as if entirely accessible to the applicant/recipient.[86]

For further information or clarification as to the rules of Medicaid as administered by the State of Rhode Island, write to:

Director
Department of Human Services
Division of Management Services
Office of Policy Development
600 New London Avenue
Cranston, RI 02920
Telephone: (401) 464-2354

SOUTH CAROLINA

The monthly income limit in determining eligibility for the Medicaid applicant/resident in a long-term health care facility/nursing home is $1,158.

The monthly income of the community spouse is not considered by Medicaid when determining the eligibility of the institutionalized spouse thirty days after he or she has entered the private nursing home facility.

The financial assets limit in determining eligibility of the Medicaid applicant residing in a long-term health care facility/nursing home is $2,000 and the usual exemptions.

The financial assets of the community spouse are currently not considered by Medicaid in determining the eligibility of the institutionalized spouse the next calendar month after he or she enters the private nursing home facility.[87]

---

[85]See page 23.

[86]See page 23.

[87]See page 23.

SURVIVING THE NOT SO GOLDEN YEARS

Joint property, as such, is treated along SSI guidelines.[88]

For further information or clarification as to the administration of Medicaid regulations for the State of South Carolina, write to:

Director
State Health and Human Services Finance Commission
P.O. Box 8206
Columbia, SC 29202-8206
Telephone: (803) 253-6142

SOUTH DAKOTA

The monthly income limit in determining eligibility for the Medicaid applicant/resident in a long-term health care facility/nursing home is $1,158.

The monthly income of the community spouse is not considered by Medicaid when determining the eligibility of the institutionalized spouse thirty days after he or she has entered the private nursing home facility.

The financial assets limit in determining eligibility of the Medicaid applicant residing in a long-term health care facility/nursing home is $2,000 and the usual exemptions.

The financial assets of the community spouse are currently not considered by Medicaid in determining the eligibility of the institutionalized spouse.[89]

Joint assets are considered totally available to the nursing home/long-term health care facility resident, unless a degree of ownership is legally defined.[90]

For further information or clarification as to the administration of Medicaid regulations for the State of South Dakota, write to:

---

[88]See page 23.

[89]See page 23.

[90]See page 23.

MEDICAID AND LONG-TERM HEALTH CARE

Director
Office of Assistance Payments
Richard F. Kneif Building
700 Governor's Drive
Pierre, SD 57501-2291
Telephone: (605) 773-4678

TENNESSEE

The monthly income limit in determining eligibility for the Medicaid applicant/resident in a long-term health care facility/nursing home is $1,158.

The monthly income of the community spouse is not considered by Medicaid when determining the eligibility of the institutionalized spouse thirty days after he or she has entered the private nursing home facility.

The financial assets limit in determining eligibility of the Medicaid applicant residing in a long-term health care facility/nursing home is $2,000 and the usual exemptions.

The financial assets of the community spouse are currently not considered by Medicaid in determining the eligibility of the institutionalized spouse.[91]

Jointly held assets which are considered countable resources are:[92]

- motor vehicles with equity value of $4,500
- cash, stocks, bonds, and bank accounts are counted in their entirety
- life insurance policies with total face value of $1,500 or less are excluded, but entire value of policy is considered if the face value exceeds $1,500
- real property that is not the homestead and that is accessible is counted
- real property with equity in excess of about $6,000

---

[91]See page 23.

[92]See page 23.

For further information or clarification as to the rules of Medicaid as administered by the State of Tennessee, write to:

Director
Department of Human Services
400 Deaderick Street
Citizens Plaza Building
Nashville, TN 37219
Telephone: (615) 741-6950
   or toll-free number is (800) 523-2863

TEXAS

The monthly income limit in determining eligibility for the Medicaid applicant/resident in a long-term health care facility/nursing home is $1,158.

The monthly income of the community spouse is not considered by Medicaid when determining the eligibility of the institutionalized spouse.

The financial assets limit in determining eligibility of the Medicaid applicant residing in a long-term health care facility/nursing home is $2,000 and the usual exemptions.

The financial assets of the community spouse are currently not considered by Medicaid in determining the eligibility of the institutionalized spouse the next calendar month after he or she enters the private nursing home facility.[93]

Joint assets which can be liquidated without legal action are considered as countable assets and 100% available to the recipient.[94]

For further information or clarification as to the rules of Medicaid as administered by the State of Texas, write to:

Director
Texas Department of Human Services

---

[93]See page 23.

[94]See page 23.

MEDICAID AND LONG-TERM HEALTH CARE

Client Eligibility Section
P.O. Box 149030
Austin, TX 78714-9030
Telephone: (512) 450-3027

UTAH

The monthly income limit in determining eligibility for the Medicaid applicant/resident in a long-term health care facility/nursing home is that it must be less than the monthly cost of the facility.

The monthly income of the community spouse is not considered by Medicaid when determining the eligibility of the institutionalized spouse thirty days after he or she has entered the private nursing home facility.

The financial assets limit in determining eligibility of the Medicaid applicant residing in a long-term health care facility/nursing home is $2,000 and the usual exemptions.

The financial assets of the community spouse are currently not considered by Medicaid in determining the eligibility of the institutionalized spouse thirty days after he or she enters the private nursing home facility.[95]

In Utah all joint assets are considered to be 100% available to each spouse but the community spouse can refute this.[96]

For further information or clarification as to the rules of Medicaid as administered by the State of Utah, write to:

Director
Division of Health Care Financing
State of Utah
Department of Health
P.O. Box 16580
Salt Lake City, UT 84116-0580
Telephone: (801) 538-6151, (801) 538-6595, or (801)538-6497

---

[95]See page 23.

[96]See page 23.

VERMONT

The monthly income limit in determining eligibility for the Medicaid applicant/resident in a long-term health care facility/nursing home is that it must be less than the monthly cost of the facility.

The monthly income of the community spouse is not considered by Medicaid when determining the eligibility of the institutionalized spouse the next calendar month after he or she enters the private nursing home facility.

The financial assets limit in determining eligibility of the Medicaid applicant residing in a long-term health care facility/nursing home is $2,000 and the usual exemptions.

The financial assets of the community spouse are currently not considered by Medicaid in determining the eligibility of the institutionalized spouse the next calendar month after he or she enters the private nursing home facility.[97]

Joint assets are handled in such a manner that if they both have access to the resources, either party can have total ownership if he or she chooses to take it.[98]

For further information or clarification as to the rules of Medicaid as administered by the State of Vermont, write to:

Director
State of Vermont
Agency of Human Services
Department of Social Welfare
103 South Main Street
Waterbury, VT 05676
Telephone: (802) 241-2800

---

[97] See page 23.

[98] See page 23.

VIRGINIA

The monthly income limit in determining eligibility for the Medicaid applicant/resident in a long-term health care facility/nursing home is $1,158.

The monthly income of the community spouse is not considered by Medicaid when determining the eligibility of the institutionalized spouse thirty days after he or she has entered the private nursing home facility.

The financial assets limit in determining eligibility of the Medicaid applicant residing in a long-term health care facility/nursing home is $2,000 and the usual exemptions.

The financial assets of the community spouse are currently not considered by Medicaid in determining the eligibility of the institutionalized spouse, provided they can be documented as belonging exclusively to the community spouse.[99]

Joint assets are considered to be equally divided between both spouses.[100]

For further information or clarification as to the rules of Medicaid as administered by the State of Virginia, write to:

Director
Virginia Department of Medical Assistance Services
600 East Broad Street
Suite 1300
Richmond, VA 23219
Telephone: (804) 786-6145

WASHINGTON

The monthly income limit in determining eligibility for the Medicaid applicant/resident in a long-term health care facility/nursing home is that it must be less than the monthly cost of the facility.

---

[99]See page 23.

[100]See page 23.

The monthly income of the community spouse is not considered by Medicaid when determining the eligibility of the institutionalized spouse.

The financial assets limit in determining eligibility of the Medicaid applicant residing in a long-term health care facility/nursing home is $2,000 and the usual exemptions.

The financial assets of the community spouse are currently not considered by Medicaid in determining the eligibility of the institutionalized spouse.[101]

Washington is one of the two states currently allowing transfer of assets between spouses without penalty. Those not transferred are considered joint or community property and one-half is assigned to each spouse.[102]

For further information or clarification as to the administering of the regulations of Medicaid by the State of Washington, write to:

Director
Office of Medical and Program Policy
Division of Medical Assistance HB-41
Department of Social and Health Services
Olympia, WA 98504-0095
Telephone: (206) 753-0526

WEST VIRGINIA

The monthly income limit in determining eligibility for the Medicaid applicant/resident in a long-term health care facility/nursing home is $1,158.

The monthly income of the community spouse is not considered by Medicaid when determining the eligibility of the institutionalized spouse.

---

[101]See page 23.

[102]See page 23.

MEDICAID AND LONG-TERM HEALTH CARE

The financial assets limit in determining eligibility of the Medicaid applicant residing in a long-term health care facility/nursing home is $2,000 and the usual exemptions.

The financial assets of the community spouse are combined with the assets of the institutionalized spouse for the first six months and cannot exceed $3,000 for the applicant to be eligible for Medicaid. After these six months, the community spouse's assets are no longer considered by Medicaid.[103]

Joint assets are considered 100% available to each spouse and a Medicaid application could be considered ineligible because of jointly held assets.[104]

For further information or clarification as to the rules of Medicaid as administered by the State of West Virginia, write to:

Director
Bureau of Income Maintenance
West Virginia Department of Health and Human
    Resources
State Capitol Building 6, Room 817
Charleston, WV 25305
Telephone: (304) 348-8290
    or toll-free number is (800) 642-8589

WISCONSIN

The monthly income limit in determining eligibility for the Medicaid applicant/resident in a long-term health care facility/nursing home is $1,158.

The maximum monthly income of the community spouse considered by Medicaid when determining the eligibility of the institutionalized spouse is $470.00. Anything in excess of this

---

[103]See page 23.

[104]See page 23.

amount can be deemed to the spouse, living in the private nursing home facility, on Medicaid.[105]

The financial assets limit in determining eligibility of the Medicaid applicant residing in a long-term health care facility/nursing home is $2,000 and the usual exemptions.

The financial assets of the community spouse are currently not considered by Medicaid in determining the eligibility of the institutionalized spouse.[106]

Joint assets are treated as totally available to the institutionalized spouse.[107]

For further information or clarification on the rules of Medicaid as administered by the State of Wisconsin, write to:

>Director
>State of Wisconsin
>Department of Health and Social Services
>Bureau of Economic Assistance
>Division of Economic Support
>Office of Welfare Reform
>1 West Wilson Street
>P.O. Box 7935
>Madison, WI 53707-7935
>Telephone: (608) 267-4525

WYOMING

The monthly income limit in determining eligibility for the Medicaid applicant/resident in a long-term health care facility/nursing home is $1,158.

The monthly income of the community spouse is not considered by Medicaid when determining the eligibility of the institutionalized spouse.

---

[105]See page 23.

[106]See page 23.

[107]See page 23.

MEDICAID AND LONG-TERM HEALTH CARE

The financial assets limit in determining eligibility of the Medicaid applicant residing in a long-term health care facility/nursing home is $2,000 and the usual exemptions.

The financial assets of the community spouse are currently not considered by Medicaid in determining the eligibility of the institutionalized spouse.[108]

Joint assets are considered available to both spouses. The recipient of Medicaid must dispose of his/her portion provided it does not force the other into disposing of his/hers. If it is impossible to liquidate without forcing the other to sell, this is considered a legal barrier and it is handled differently.[109]

For further information or clarification as to the rules of Medicaid as administered by the State of Wyoming, write to:

Director
Department of Health & Social Services
Division of Public Assistance & Social Services
Hathaway Building, 3rd Floor
Cheyenne, WY 82002
Telephone: (307) 777-6079

---

[108]See page 23.

[109]See page 23.

PART TWO

Long-Term Health Care Facilities

Chapter 5

WHY IT IS IMPORTANT FOR YOU TO KNOW ABOUT NURSING HOME FACILITIES

The reader may ask, why is it important for me to know all these facts about Medicaid and nursing homes unless someone very close to me or someone I know is imminently in need of this information. The answer is—being armed with the knowledge of these facts will better prepare you to handle what could be a very difficult and costly situation.

For example, take the case of an elderly woman afflicted with Alzheimer's Disease who was asked to leave the nursing home where she had been a resident, even though she was in the process of applying for Medicaid. She was asked to leave because of her inability to pay and her family had already exhausted all their funds, including personal loans, to cover her expenses.

In this particular case, had the family made application to Medicaid for their mother, she would have been able to spend down or exhaust her funds by paying the cost of the nursing home. Then she would have been able to meet eligibility requirements for Medicaid in time to have Medicaid assume the cost of the nursing home. With prior knowledge and a

SURVIVING THE NOT SO GOLDEN YEARS

basic understanding of the Medicaid eligibility requirements, this whole unfortunate incident could have been avoided.

Before presenting the information on nursing homes relevant to their participation in Medicaid, it is important to cover some general information on this topic. Here are some thoughts and circumstances to be aware of and to consider when trying to make that most painful decision on whether it is in the best interest of a loved one for him or her to be in a good nursing home. Following are (page 82, etc.) some suggestions on how to locate a good nursing home and how to evaluate them in order to determine if a particular facility is satisfactory and suitable to your needs.

WHEN AND WHY YOU SHOULD CONSIDER A NURSING HOME FACILITY

"I will never put my mother (father, sister, brother) in a nursing home."

These words, I'm sure, echo in the hearts and minds of all family members faced with the dilemma of what to do with aging parents or siblings. The scenario can be any one of the following:

- parents who are sound of mind, but getting on in years, and who have difficulty managing a normal household
- a widowed parent who wishes to maintain his or her autonomy and independence, but who is living alone, which causes concern for his or her family
- a parent who, because of his or her desire to remain at home, has chosen to have a live-in companion
- a person whose mental faculties are failing or becoming seriously impaired due to aging and illness
- a person who is seriously handicapped or becoming physically debilitated due to aging and illness
- a person whose family lives at such a great distance as to cause his or her family concern because he or she also falls into one of the above categories

LONG-TERM HEALTH CARE FACILITIES

Relevant to these scenarios are the following issues:

(1) Is the parent (or parents) still able to carry on the everyday functions of daily living, i.e., shopping, going out, managing alone on public transportation, driving alone, meeting friends, coming home alone—perhaps after dark, etc.
(2) Does the aging parent have friends? Is just coping alone a major part of their existence? Do they have occasion to interact with others socially or through groups and organizations?
(3) Are they physically near or in touch with someone who can be there for them immediately in time of crisis? Do they have a medical support system—or a hotline number to call in case of emergency?

All these factors are issues that must be faced when evaluating what is best for your parents or loved ones in their golden years—provided this decision is yours to make and provided to some extent they are willing to let you make it. Therefore, let us examine the "nursing home solution." Provided a good nursing home is chosen with great care and is suitable for your needs, some of the positive aspects can be:

(1) The person you care about is no longer isolated.
(2) He/she no longer has to be responsible for cooking, cleaning, shopping, and caring for a household, etc. All meals will be provided.
(3) He/she will be spared the possibility of being totally alone in case of a medical emergency.
(4) He/she will be afforded the services of a caring and skilled staff, if need be.
(5) He/she will have the opportunity of making friends and associating with peers on at least a daily, if not on a more frequent basis.

These advantages do not mean that a nursing home is always the only solution, but they certainly indicate that a nursing home should not necessarily be ruled out. These points deserve consideration also because sometimes the nursing home option is in reality the only one.

ISSUES TO CONSIDER WHEN SELECTING A NURSING HOME FACILITY

Legal Protection for Medicaid Patients

The following are two of the most important basic federal regulations[1] that govern all nursing homes participating in the Medicaid program and that are most frequently violated by nursing homes themselves:

(1) No nursing home, participating in Medicaid, can require that a person seeking entrance into a nursing home, has lived in that state, county, or city prior to admission—A DURATIONAL RESIDENCY REQUIREMENT IS ILLEGAL. (See Glossary.)
(2) No nursing home participating in the Medicaid program can discriminate in any manner, such as inferior accommodations, designating a specific location in the home as a Medicaid wing, or other discrepancies, including attitude and manner of treatment, etc., because of financial status. What the regulations state is that all residents MUST BE TREATED EQUALLY—BOTH MEDICAID AND PRIVATE PAYING.

Locating a Nursing Home or Homes

(1) Call or write to the office listed in the state[2] of your choice provided in this book.
(2) Check with senior citizen groups, church groups, or your physician.
(3) Check with the Department of Health for your state. (They must license all nursing homes.)

---

[1] These rules are found in Federal Regulations 42 CFR 435.403(j)(1), 42 CFR 430.0(b)(2)(ii) (residency) and (financial) 45 CFR 80 and 84.

[2] Remember that it is against the law to require *previous* residency in a state as a qualification for Medicaid in a nursing home.

(4) Check with your local Social Security Office.
(5) Check the yellow pages of your telephone directory.

Financial Issues

(1) What is the annual rate for a skilled nursing facility (if needed)?
(2) What is the annual rate for an intermediate-care facility (if needed)?
(3) What other expenses are involved, such as the cost of a special mattress or a wheelchair if needed, physical therapist, hairdresser or barber, etc?
(4) Do they accept Medicare/Medicaid? (Remember the percentage of private insurance companies covering nursing homes is negligible.) *This information is crucial.*
(5) Can the resident make the transition from private payment to Medicaid without being evicted?
(6) Will they offer assistance or counselling when and if the time comes to apply for Medicaid?

Evaluating the Nursing Home

Inquire about, or investigate personally:

(1) *Cleanliness.* There should be no unpleasant sustained odors; the condition of the residents (appearance, clothing, etc.) should be clean.
(2) *Furniture.* It should be neat, clean, presentable, and sturdy. No sharp corners or edges.
(3) *Hallways.* These should be clean, well lighted, and have grip railings. There should be no loose rugs or carelessly placed furniture.
(4) *Dining Room and Meals.* These should be clean, pleasant; meals should include at least one hot meal at noon, the diet well balanced. (Residents needing help should receive assistance.) Dining rooms should have supervised dining.
(5) *Kitchen.* It should be clean and well lighted, as well as approved or licensed by Board of Health or Department of Health. The kitchen should be able to respond to special

dietary needs, i.e., low sodium, low cholesterol, low fat, soft diet, diabetic diet, etc.

(6) *Toilet Facilities*. These should be designed specifically to accommodate wheelchair residents, including a handrail near the toilet; there also should be showers with *seats*, and of course hot and cold running water.

(7) *Recreation Room*. It should be pleasant and offer a gathering place for residents and visitors. There should be designated smoking and non-smoking areas. (Inquiries should be made of the administrator as to what activity programs are available and how they are conducted.)

(8) *Bedrooms*. These should be pleasant and airy. They should all have windows and open into corridors. Each bedroom should also contain, with easy access for the residents, the following: a nurse call-device; fresh drinking water; access to a privacy screen; reading light close to bed; and a separate closet and drawers for personal belongings.

(9) *Auxiliary Services*. These should include a hairdresser, barber, library, laundry facilities, and transportation to nearby community, etc.

(10) *Grounds*. The residents should be encouraged to enjoy going outdoors—when weather and ground conditions permit. Volunteers or staff assistants should be available to assist residents who cannot go outdoors by themselves.

(11) *Fire Safety*. All exits and all access to exits should be clearly and carefully marked and should never be blocked or locked on the inside.

Medical Services

Inquire about, or personally investigate, the following:

(1) Is there an attending physician on call for emergencies?
(2) Can the family retain their own physician should they so desire?
(3) Is the intensity, or degree, of medical service necessary for the sustained health care of your loved one, available at all times?

(4) Are there available the services of other members of the medical community such as a dentist, podiatrist, and optometrist?
(5) Is there any arrangement with a nearby hospital in case of serious illness?
(6) If there is a need, is the nursing home equipped to provide rehabilitation services and can the services of a physical therapist be engaged?

Personal Needs

Also investigate:

(1) Visiting privileges—can family and friends visit easily?
(2) Is the staff friendly, cheerful, alert, and willing to answer all questions?
(3) Is the administration helpful and cooperative in assisting with the difficult process of admissions, answering all questions willingly and efficiently?
(4) Is there a spirit of open communication between staff and residents?
(5) Is there a good ratio of staff to residents?

An example of a good ratio of staff (care-givers as opposed to administrators) to residents would be:

- *ideal*—six to one (six residents for one care-giver)
- *acceptable*—eight to one (eight residents to one care-giver)
- *not good*—twelve to one (twelve residents to one care-giver)

In most cases, the responsibility of twelve or more residents for one care-giver is too great a number to allow for the care-giver to provide the level of health care needed for his or her patients.

Chapter 6

IMPORTANT FACTS THAT YOU SHOULD KNOW

The following general information on nursing homes is not intended to be an exhaustive study. It is intended to spare the reader from having to comb through pages and pages of technical evaluations on these facilities. It is meant to provide, in a few simple paragraphs, vital information about nursing homes in general and their relationship to Medicaid in each state. The reason for focusing primarily on nursing homes and their relationship to Medicaid is that no matter how well-intentioned people are about their loved-ones, there may come a time when the money is no longer available to care for the person in the nursing home and the only alternative left is to seek financial assistance through Medicaid. At that time, knowledge of the following facts will be important to know:

BASIC FACTS ABOUT NURSING HOMES

(1) All reputable nursing home facilities must be licensed by the Department of Health in the state where they are located.
(2) All reputable nursing home facilities wishing to participate in Medicaid must apply for a certificate to do so. The state makes the determination to grant this certificate to participate

LONG-TERM HEALTH CARE FACILITIES

in Medicaid to the nursing home based on demonstrable need, such as statistical information on aged and needy population in a certain demographic area, number of facilities, etc. In most states, that determination falls within a process called Certificate of Need. Part of the process allocates the number or percentage of beds the nursing home facility may reserve for Medicaid patients.

(3) The total number of private nursing home facilities in your state—(the maximum number of facilities from which you can choose, not including facilities owned and operated by the state or county).

(4) The percentage of the total number of these facilities participating in Medicaid—(approximately how many facilities there are, from which you should choose, should you anticipate the possibility of needing financial assistance in the form of Medicaid).

Generally speaking, Medicaid works according to the following formula.[1] If a nursing home facility has 100 beds, only 40 of those 100 may be allotted for Medicaid patients. There should not be 40 actual beds set aside only for Medicaid patients, but that figure does represent a fixed number which cannot be changed at will by the nursing home. As was previously stated, the number of Medicaid patients which the nursing home facility must accept is determined by the state's Certificate of Need division. What occurs when a private paying patient runs out of funds and, no longer able to pay the cost of the nursing home, needs to apply for Medicaid? It is then necessary for the nursing home to find him or her an available bed among the forty-bed allotment for Medicaid patients, as he or she no longer falls into the category of private paying patient and can no longer be considered part of the private bed allotment.

This whole situation can become a very unpleasant, if not a disastrous experience, for the family of the resident in the nursing home facility. As you will see later on, in some states

---

[1] These numbers and percentages are not factual figures but are only representative for the sake of this example.

the facility can go so far as to evict the patient for an inability to pay, returning him or her to the family. Therefore, it is to everyone's benefit to at least be aware of the rules and regulations governing nursing home facilities in your state.

(5) The average rate or cost of the facility both on a per diem and annual basis. In all states, the figures will vary slightly depending on such factors as whether the level of care is skilled or intermediate. The figures will give you a general idea of the amount of finances involved in resolving your particular situation.

(6) The attitude of how the majority of nursing homes handle the transition of a patient from paying privately to receiving Medicaid is reflected in the last statement for each state. However, the actual details of how this financial transition is made and exactly when Medicaid assumes payments is up to the local Medicaid office and the individual nursing home. But it is also the responsibility of all parties—the family of the applicant, the Medicaid office, and the nursing home—to find out and share this information, to avoid any painful and costly misunderstandings.

(7) Finally, it is important to know whether the nursing home in your state has the power to evict a resident for the inability to pay, even while he or she is applying for Medicaid, or if that resident is protected by law, as in some states, from such action. Also, it would be very helpful to know how the nursing home handles this period of financial transition. Do they provide counseling for the person or the family responsible for the resident, advising them as to when is the appropriate time to apply for Medicaid? Will they offer assistance in financing another suitable facility, should they have no available beds?

NURSING HOME POLICIES
TOWARD MEDICAID STATE BY STATE

The following pages contain the information you need to know for each of the 50 states. This information will provide helpful input in finding the appropriate nursing home, one where you can feel secure in the knowledge that your loved one will be well cared for, regardless of his or her financial situation:

LONG-TERM HEALTH CARE FACILITIES

ALABAMA

- All private nursing home facilities in the State of Alabama can elect to participate in Medicaid provided they are licensed and certified to do so.
- The total number of private nursing home facilities in the State of Alabama, including skilled nursing facilities and intermediate care facilities, is approximately 215.
- The percentage of this total number of private nursing home facilities in the State of Alabama participating in Medicaid is approximately 94.3 percent.
- The current occupancy rate for private nursing home facilities in the State of Alabama is approximately 93.3 percent. This number is a statewide average and varies slightly from facility to facility.
- The average rate for a private paying resident in a private nursing home facility in the State of Alabama is approximately $60 per diem, or approximately $21,900 annually. This rate may vary slightly, depending upon whether the facility is a skilled nursing care or intermediate nursing care facility.

A private paying resident in a private nursing home facility in the State of Alabama, participating in Medicaid, can apply for Medicaid while still in the facility even after his or her funds are exhausted. But it is up to the discretion of the nursing home whether he or she can remain there and all that is required is 30 days notice before asking that person to leave.

For further information on nursing homes and Medicaid in the State of Alabama call (205) 277-2710 (or write to address given for Alabama in the Medicaid Section).

ALASKA

- All private nursing home facilities in the State of Alaska can elect to participate in Medicaid provided they are licensed and certified to do so.
- The total number of private nursing home facilities in the State of Alaska, including skilled nursing facilities and intermediate care facilities, is approximately 15.

- The percentage of this total number of private nursing home facilities in the State of Alaska participating in Medicaid is approximately 90 percent.
- The current occupancy rate for private nursing home facilities in the State of Alaska is approximately 90 percent. This number is a statewide average and varies slightly from facility to facility.
- The average rate for a private paying resident in a private nursing home facility in the State of Alaska is approximately $170 per diem, or approximately $62,000 annually. This rate may vary slightly, depending upon whether the facility is a skilled nursing care or intermediate nursing care facility.

There are some private free-standing nursing homes where one of the requirements for admission is being a resident of Alaska for 15 years or more. Fortunately, this regulation is prohibited by Federal law for all private nursing homes participating in Medicaid and, therefore, cannot apply to Medicaid applicants or residents. Also, private paying residents in a private nursing home facility participating in Medicaid cannot be asked to leave or be transferred after their funds have been exhausted, provided they are applying for Medicaid.

For further information on nursing homes and Medicaid in the State of Alaska call (907) 465-3355 (or write to address given for Alaska in the Medicaid Section).

ARIZONA

- All private nursing home facilities in the State of Arizona can elect to participate in Medicaid/AHCCCS[2] provided they are licensed and certified to do so.

---

[2]AHCCCS refers to the State of Arizona's health program, equivalent to Medicaid. The initials stand for Arizona Health Care Cost Containment System (the state's health care program for the needy). There is also a program referred to as ALTCS—Arizona Long Term Care System.

LONG-TERM HEALTH CARE FACILITIES

- The total number of private nursing home facilities in the State of Arizona, including skilled nursing facilities and intermediate-care facilities, is approximately 130.
- The percentage of this total number of private nursing home facilities in the State of Arizona, participating in Medicaid/AHCCCS is approximately 62 percent.
- The current occupancy rate for private nursing home facilities in the State of Arizona is approximately 75 percent. This number is a statewide average and varies slightly from facility to facility.
- The average rate for a private paying resident in a private nursing home facility in the State of Arizona is approximately $62 per diem, or approximately $22,630 annually. This rate may vary slightly depending upon whether the facility is a skilled nursing care or intermediate nursing care facility.

In the State of Arizona, private paying residents in a private nursing home facility participating in Medicaid/AHCCCS are not protected by law from being evicted after their funds have been exhausted, even though they have applied for Medicaid/AHCCCS. The decision as to how long they can remain is left to the discretion of the individual facility.

For further information on nursing homes and Medicaid/AHCCCS in the State of Arizona call (602) 220-6405 (or write to address given for Arizona in the Medicaid Section).

ARKANSAS

- All private nursing home facilities in the State of Arkansas can elect to participate in Medicaid provided they are licensed and certified to do so.
- The total number of private nursing home facilities in the State of Arkansas, including skilled nursing facilities and intermediate-care facilities, is approximately 218.
- The percentage of this total number of private nursing home facilities in the State of Arkansas participating in Medicaid is approximately 100 percent.

- The current occupancy rate for private nursing home facilities in the State of Arkansas is approximately 93 percent. This number is a statewide average and varies slightly from facility to facility.
- The average rate for a private paying resident in a private nursing home facility in the State of Arkansas is approximately $30 per diem, or approximately $16,425 annually. This rate may vary slightly, depending upon whether the facility is a skilled nursing care or intermediate nursing care facility.

In the State of Arkansas, private paying residents in a private nursing home facility participating in Medicaid cannot be asked to leave or be transferred when their funds have been exhausted, provided they are applying for Medicaid. Also, in the majority of cases in Arkansas, the nursing home is aware of the status of the resident and is prepared to help him/her apply for Medicaid.

For further information on nursing homes and Medicaid in the State of Arkansas call (501) 682-8470 (or write to address given for Arkansas in the Medicaid Section).

CALIFORNIA

- All private nursing home facilities in the State of California can elect to participate in Medicaid/Medi-Cal[3] provided they are licensed and certified to do so.
- The total number of private nursing home facilities in the State of California, including skilled nursing facilities and intermediate-care facilities, is approximately 1,357.
- The percentage of this total number of private nursing home facilities in the State of California participating in Medicaid/Medi-Cal is approximately 99 percent.
- The current occupancy rate for private nursing home facilities in the State of California is approximately 98 percent. This

---

[3] Medi-Cal is the state of California's health program, equivalent to Medicaid.

number is a statewide average and varies slightly from facility to facility.
- The average rate for a private paying resident in a private nursing home facility in the State of California is approximately $50 per diem, or approximately $18,250 annually. This rate may vary slightly, depending upon whether the facility is a skilled nursing care or intermediate nursing care facility.

In the State of California, private paying residents in a private nursing home facility participating in Medicaid/Medi-Cal cannot be asked to leave or be transferred when their funds have been exhausted, provided they are applying for Medicaid/Medi-Cal.

For further information on nursing homes and Medicaid/Medi-Cal in the State of California call (916) 324-2499 (or write to address given for California in the Medicaid Section).

COLORADO

- All private nursing home facilities in the State of Colorado can elect to participate in Medicaid provided they are licensed and certified to do so.
- The total number of private nursing home facilities in the State of Colorado, including skilled nursing facilities and intermediate-care facilities, is approximately 176.
- The percentage of this total number of private nursing home facilities in the State of Colorado participating in Medicaid is approximately 100 percent.
- The current occupancy rate for private nursing home facilities in the State of Colorado is approximately 87 percent. This number is a statewide average and varies slightly from facility to facility.
- The average rate for a private paying resident in a private nursing home facility in the State of Colorado is approximately $49 per diem, or approximately $17,885 annually. This rate may vary slightly, depending upon whether the facility is a skilled nursing care or intermediate nursing care facility.

In the State of Colorado, private paying residents in a private nursing home facility participating in Medicaid cannot be asked to leave or be transferred when their funds have been exhausted, provided they are applying for Medicaid.

For further information on nursing homes and Medicaid in the State of Colorado call (303) 866-2430 (or write to address given for Colorado in the Medicaid Section).

CONNECTICUT

- All private nursing home facilities in the State of Connecticut can elect to participate in Medicaid provided they are licensed and certified to do so.
- The total number of private nursing home facilities in the State of Connecticut, including skilled nursing facilities and intermediate-care facilities, is approximately 370.
- The percentage of this total number of private nursing home facilities in the State of Connecticut participating in Medicaid is approximately 100 percent, as determined by Certificate of Need process.
- The current occupancy rate for private nursing home facilities in the State of Connecticut is approximately 95 percent. This number is a statewide average and varies slightly from facility to facility.
- The average rate for a private paying resident in a private nursing home facility in the State of Connecticut is approximately $84 per diem, or approximately $30,660 annually. This rate may vary slightly, depending upon whether the facility is a skilled nursing care or intermediate nursing care facility.

In the State of Connecticut, private paying residents in a private nursing home facility participating in Medicaid cannot be asked to leave or be transferred when their funds have been exhausted, provided they are applying for Medicaid.

In Connecticut all nursing homes participating in the Medicaid Program are bound by the "Waiting List Law" which states, in effect, that all applicants for these nursing home facilities must put their names on a waiting list—both private paying and Medicaid applicants—and by law they *must be accepted* into the facility based on their date of application and in chronological order and not by order of private paying applicants over Medicaid applicants.

For further information on nursing homes and Medicaid in the State of Connecticut call (203) 566-2019 (or write to address given for Connecticut in the Medicaid Section).

DELAWARE

- All private nursing home facilities in the State of Delaware can elect to participate in Medicaid provided they are licensed and certified to do so.
- The total number of private nursing home facilities in the State of Delaware, including skilled nursing facilities and intermediate-care facilities, is approximately 55.
- The percentage of this total number of private nursing home facilities in the State of Delaware participating in Medicaid is approximately 100 percent.
- The current occupancy rate for private nursing home facilities in the State of Delaware is approximately 98 percent. This number is a statewide average and varies slightly from facility to facility.
- The average rate for a private paying resident in a private nursing home facility in the State of Delaware is approximately $85 per diem, or approximately $31,025 annually. This rate may vary slightly, depending upon whether the facility is a skilled nursing care or intermediate nursing care facility.

In the State of Delaware, private paying residents in a private nursing home facility participating in Medicaid cannot be asked to leave or be transferred when their funds have been exhausted, provided they are applying for Medicaid.

For further information on nursing homes and Medicaid in the State of Delaware call (302) 421-6299 (or write to address given for Delaware in the Medicaid Section).

DISTRICT OF COLUMBIA

- All private nursing home facilities in the District of Columbia can elect to participate in Medicaid provided they are licensed and certified to do so.
- The total number of private nursing home facilities in the District of Columbia, including skilled nursing facilities and intermediate-care facilities, is approximately 13.
- The percentage of this total number of private nursing home facilities in the District of Columbia participating in Medicaid is approximately 100 percent.
- The current occupancy rate for private nursing home facilities in the District of Columbia is approximately 93 percent. This number is a District average and varies slightly from facility to facility.
- The average rate for a private paying resident in a private nursing home facility in the District of Columbia is approximately $100 per diem, or approximately $36,500 annually. This rate may vary slightly, depending upon whether the facility is a skilled nursing care or intermediate nursing care facility.

In the District of Columbia, private paying residents in a private nursing home facility participating in Medicaid cannot be asked to leave or be transferred when their funds have been exhausted, provided they are applying for Medicaid.

For further information on nursing homes and Medicaid in the District of Columbia, call (202) 727-0735 (or write to address given for Washington, D.C., in the Medicaid Section).

FLORIDA

- All private nursing home facilities in the State of Florida can elect to participate in Medicaid provided they are licensed and certified to do so.
- The total number of private nursing home facilities in the State of Florida, including skilled nursing facilities and intermediate-care facilities, is approximately 500.

LONG-TERM HEALTH CARE FACILITIES

- The percentage of this total number of private nursing home facilities in the State of Florida participating in Medicaid is approximately 80 percent.
- The current occupancy rate for private nursing home facilities in the State of Florida is approximately 98 percent. This number is a statewide average and varies slightly from facility to facility.
- The average rate for a private paying resident in a private nursing home facility in the State of Florida is approximately $67 per diem, or approximately $24,555 annually. This rate may vary slightly, depending upon whether the facility is a skilled nursing care or intermediate nursing care facility.

In the State of Florida, private paying residents in a private nursing home facility participating in Medicaid cannot be asked to leave or be transferred when their funds have been exhausted, provided they are applying for Medicaid.

For further information on nursing homes and Medicaid in the State of Florida call (904) 488-9990 (or write to address given for Florida in the Medicaid Section).

GEORGIA

- All private nursing home facilities in the State of Georgia can elect to participate in Medicaid provided they are licensed and certified to do so.
- The total number of private nursing home facilities in the State of Georgia, including skilled nursing facilities and intermediate-care facilities, is approximately 354.
- The percentage of this total number of private nursing home facilities in the State of Georgia participating in Medicaid is approximately 90 percent.
- The current occupancy rate for private nursing home facilities in the State of Georgia is approximately 96 percent. This number is a statewide average and varies slightly from facility to facility.
- The average rate for a private paying resident in a private nursing home facility in the State of Georgia is approximately $47 per diem, or approximately $16,995 annually. This rate may

vary slightly, depending upon whether the facility is a skilled nursing care or intermediate nursing care facility.

In a private nursing home facility which participates in Medicaid in the State of Georgia, a private paying patient who has exhausted his or her funds and must apply for Medicaid can avoid any possibility of being asked to leave for lack of payment by being pre-certified for Medicaid. This is accomplished by filling out a specific form which is signed by a physician and filed with the Georgia Medical Care Foundation. When the time comes to apply for Medicaid, the form is retrieved and it automatically provides the necessary information for Medicaid approval. Most states do not have this provision.

For further information on nursing homes and Medicaid in the State of Georgia call (404) 656-4273 (or write to address given for Georgia in the Medicaid Section).

HAWAII

- All private nursing home facilities in the State of Hawaii can elect to participate in Medicaid provided they are licensed and certified to do so.
- The total number of private nursing home facilities in the State of Hawaii, including skilled nursing facilities and intermediate-care facilities, is approximately 12.
- The percentage of this total number of private nursing home facilities in the State of Hawaii participating in Medicaid is approximately 99 percent.
- The current occupancy rate for private nursing home facilities in the State of Hawaii is approximately 97 percent. This number is a statewide average and varies slightly from facility to facility.
- The average rate for a private paying resident in a private nursing home facility in the State of Hawaii is approximately $92 per diem, or approximately $33,580 annually. This rate may vary slightly, depending upon whether the facility is a skilled nursing care or intermediate nursing care facility.

In the State of Hawaii, private paying residents in a private nursing home facility participating in Medicaid cannot be asked to leave or be transferred when their funds have been exhausted, provided they are applying for Medicaid.

For further information on nursing homes and Medicaid in the State of Hawaii call (808) 548-6584 (or write to address given for Hawaii in the Medicaid Section).

IDAHO

- All private nursing home facilities in the State of Idaho can elect to participate in Medicaid provided they are licensed and certified to do so.
- The total number of private nursing home facilities in the State of Idaho, including skilled nursing facilities and intermediate-care facilities, is approximately 44.
- The percentage of this total number of private nursing home facilities in the State of Idaho participating in Medicaid is approximately 62 percent.
- The current occupancy rate for private nursing home facilities in the State of Idaho is approximately 92 percent. This number is a statewide average and varies slightly from facility to facility.
- The average rate for a private paying resident in a private nursing home facility in the State of Idaho is approximately $57 per diem, or approximately $20,805 annually. This rate may vary slightly, depending upon whether the facility is a skilled nursing care or intermediate nursing care facility.

In the State of Idaho, private paying residents in a private nursing home facility participating in Medicaid cannot be asked to leave or be transferred when their funds have been exhausted, provided they are applying for Medicaid.

For further information on nursing homes and Medicaid in the State of Idaho call (208) 334-5795 (or write to address given for Idaho in the Medicaid Section).

ILLINOIS

- All private nursing home facilities in the State of Illinois can elect to participate in Medicaid provided they are licensed and certified to do so.
- The total number of private nursing home facilities in the State of Illinois, including skilled nursing facilities and intermediate-care facilities, is approximately 693.
- The percentage of this total number of private nursing home facilities in the State of Illinois participating in Medicaid is approximately 100 percent.
- The current occupancy rate for private nursing home facilities in the State of Illinois is approximately 80 percent. This number is a statewide average and varies slightly from facility to facility.
- The average rate for a private paying resident in a private nursing home facility in the State of Illinois is approximately $60 per diem, or approximately $21,900 annually. This rate may vary slightly, depending upon whether the facility is a skilled nursing care or intermediate nursing care facility.

In the State of Illinois, private paying residents in a private nursing home facility participating in Medicaid cannot be asked to leave or be transferred when their funds have been exhausted, provided they are applying for Medicaid.

For further information on nursing homes and Medicaid in the State of Illinois call (217) 782-0545 (or write to address given for Illinois in the Medicaid Section).

INDIANA

- All private nursing home facilities in the State of Indiana can elect to participate in Medicaid provided they are licensed and certified to do so.
- The total number of private nursing home facilities in the State of Indiana, including skilled nursing facilities and intermediate-care facilities, is approximately 625.

LONG-TERM HEALTH CARE FACILITIES

● The percentage of this total number of private nursing home facilities in the State of Indiana participating in Medicaid is approximately 83 percent.
● The current occupancy rate for private nursing home facilities in the State of Indiana is approximately 84 percent. This number is a statewide average and varies slightly from facility to facility.
● The average rate for a private paying resident in a private nursing home facility in the State of Indiana is approximately $80 per diem, or approximately $29,200 annually. This rate may vary slightly, depending upon whether the facility is a skilled nursing care or intermediate nursing care facility.

In the State of Indiana, private paying residents in a private nursing home facility participating in Medicaid cannot be asked to leave or be transferred when their funds have been exhausted, provided they are applying for Medicaid.
For further information on nursing homes and Medicaid in the State of Indiana call (317) 232-4369 (or write to address given for Indiana in the Medicaid Section).

IOWA

● All private nursing home facilities in the State of Iowa can elect to participate in Medicaid provided they are licensed and certified to do so.
● The total number of private nursing home facilities in the State of Iowa, including skilled nursing facilities and intermediate-care facilities, is approximately 431.
● The percentage of this total number of private nursing home facilities in the State of Iowa participating in Medicaid is approximately 100 percent.
● The current occupancy rate for private nursing home facilities in the State of Iowa is approximately 94 percent. This number is a statewide average and varies slightly from facility to facility.
● The average rate for a private paying resident in a private nursing home facility in the State of Iowa is approximately $40 per diem, or approximately $14,600 annually. This rate may

vary slightly, depending upon whether the facility is a skilled nursing care or intermediate nursing care facility.

In the State of Iowa, private paying residents in a private nursing home facility participating in Medicaid cannot be asked to leave or be transferred when their funds have been exhausted, provided they are applying for Medicaid.

For further information on nursing homes and Medicaid in the State of Iowa call (515) 281-8621 or (515) 270-1198 (or write to address given for Iowa in the Medicaid Section).

KANSAS

- All private nursing home facilities in the State of Kansas can elect to participate in Medicaid provided they are licensed and certified to do so.
- The total number of private nursing home facilities in the State of Kansas, including skilled nursing facilities and intermediate-care facilities, is approximately 400.
- The percentage of this total number of private nursing home facilities in the State of Kansas participating in Medicaid is approximately 50 percent.
- The current occupancy rate for private nursing home facilities in the State of Kansas is approximately 91 percent. This number is a statewide average and varies slightly from facility to facility.
- The average rate for a private paying resident in a private nursing home facility in the State of Kansas is approximately $68 per diem, or approximately $25,000 annually. This rate may vary slightly, depending upon whether the facility is a skilled nursing care or intermediate nursing care facility.

In the State of Kansas, private paying residents in a private nursing home facility participating in Medicaid cannot be asked to leave or be transferred when their funds have been exhausted, provided they are applying for Medicaid.

For further information on nursing homes and Medicaid in the State of Kansas call (913) 296-3728 (or write to address given for Kansas in the Medicaid Section).

LONG-TERM HEALTH CARE FACILITIES

KENTUCKY

- All private nursing home facilities in the State of Kentucky can elect to participate in Medicaid provided they are licensed and certified to do so.
- The total number of private nursing home facilities in the State of Kentucky, including skilled nursing facilities and intermediate-care facilities, is approximately 306.
- The percentage of this total number of private nursing home facilities in the State of Kentucky participating in Medicaid is approximately 98 percent.
- The current occupancy rate for private nursing home facilities in the State of Kentucky is approximately 95 percent. This number is a statewide average and varies slightly from facility to facility.
- The average rate for a private paying resident in a private nursing home facility in the State of Kentucky is approximately $70 per diem, or approximately $25,550 annually. This rate may vary slightly, depending upon whether the facility is a skilled nursing care or intermediate nursing care facility.

In the State of Kentucky, private paying residents in a private nursing home facility participating in Medicaid cannot be asked to leave or be transferred when their funds have been exhausted, provided they are applying for Medicaid.

For further information on nursing homes and Medicaid in the State of Kentucky call (502) 564-2800 (or write to address given for Kentucky in the Medicaid Section).

LOUISIANA

- All private nursing home facilities in the State of Louisiana can elect to participate in Medicaid provided they are licensed and certified to do so.
- The total number of private nursing home facilities in the State of Louisiana, including skilled nursing facilities and intermediate-care facilities, is approximately 281.

SURVIVING THE NOT SO GOLDEN YEARS

- The percentage of this total number of private nursing home facilities in the State of Louisiana participating in Medicaid is approximately 90 percent.
- The current occupancy rate for private nursing home facilities in the State of Louisiana is approximately 87 percent. This number is a statewide average and varies slightly from facility to facility.
- The average rate for a private paying resident in a private nursing home facility in the State of Louisiana is approximately $50 per diem, or approximately $18,250 annually. This rate may vary slightly, depending upon whether the facility is a skilled nursing care or intermediate nursing care facility.

In the State of Louisiana, private paying residents in a private nursing home facility participating in Medicaid can be asked to leave or be transferred for inability to pay when their funds have been exhausted, even though they have applied for Medicaid. This decision is left to the discretion of the individual facility.

For further information on nursing homes and Medicaid in the State of Louisiana call (504) 342-3895 (or write to address given for Louisiana in the Medicaid Section).

MAINE

- All private nursing home facilities in the State of Maine can elect to participate in Medicaid provided they are licensed and certified to do so.
- The total number of private nursing home facilities in the State of Maine, including skilled nursing facilities and intermediate-care facilities, is approximately 175.
- The percentage of this total number of private nursing home facilities in the State of Maine participating in Medicaid is approximately 100 percent.
- The current occupancy rate for private nursing home facilities in the State of Maine is approximately 90 percent. This number is a statewide average and varies slightly from facility to facility.

LONG-TERM HEALTH CARE FACILITIES

- The average rate for a private paying resident in a private nursing home facility in the State of Maine is approximately $70 per diem, or approximately $25,550 annually. This rate may vary slightly, depending upon whether the facility is a skilled nursing care or intermediate nursing care facility.

In the State of Maine, private paying residents in a private nursing home facility participating in Medicaid cannot be asked to leave or be transferred when their funds have been exhausted, provided they are applying for Medicaid.

For further information on nursing homes and Medicaid in the State of Maine call (207) 289-2674 (or write to address given for Maine in the Medicaid Section).

MARYLAND

- All private nursing home facilities in the State of Maryland can elect to participate in Medicaid provided they are licensed and certified to do so.
- The total number of private nursing home facilities in the State of Maryland, including skilled nursing facilities and intermediate-care facilities, is approximately 201.
- The percentage of this total number of private nursing home facilities in the State of Maryland participating in Medicaid is approximately 65 percent.
- The current occupancy rate for private nursing home facilities in the State of Maryland is approximately 99 percent. This number is a statewide average and varies slightly from facility to facility.
- The average rate for a private paying resident in a private nursing home facility in the State of Maryland is approximately $70 per diem, or approximately $25,550 annually. This rate may vary slightly, depending upon whether the facility is a skilled nursing care or intermediate nursing care facility.

In the State of Maryland, private paying residents in a private nursing home facility participating in Medicaid cannot be asked to leave or be transferred when their funds have been exhausted, provided they are applying for Medicaid.

For further information on nursing homes and Medicaid in the State of Maryland call (301) 225-1444 (or write to address given for Maryland in the Medicaid Section).

MASSACHUSETTS

- All private nursing home facilities in the State of Massachusetts can elect to participate in Medicaid provided they are licensed and certified to do so.
- The total number of private nursing home facilities in the State of Massachusetts, including skilled nursing facilities and intermediate-care facilities, is approximately 561.
- The percentage of this total number of private nursing home facilities in the State of Massachusetts participating in Medicaid is approximately 87 percent.
- The current occupancy rate for private nursing home facilities in the State of Massachusetts is approximately 96 percent. This number is a statewide average and varies slightly from facility to facility.
- The average rate for a private paying resident in a private nursing home facility in the State of Massachusetts is approximately $85 per diem, or approximately $31,025 annually. This rate may vary slightly, depending upon whether the facility is a skilled nursing care or intermediate nursing care facility.

The State of Massachusetts has in place a pre-screening program for all nursing home applicants which, in effect, looks at the medical and financial condition of the applicant and pre-determines: (1) whether the applicant is in need of a nursing home or would be better served by an alternative called Home-Care; and (2) if so, when the applicant's funds are exhausted, whether he/she will be acceptable for Medicaid, and/or a Public Assistance Program which also funds Home-Care. This pre-screening process enables the applicant to transfer smoothly from private payment to Medicaid or Public Assistance.

For further information on nursing homes and Medicaid in the State of Massachusetts call (617) 326-8967 (or write to address given for Massachusetts in the Medicaid Section).

LONG-TERM HEALTH CARE FACILITIES

MICHIGAN

- All private nursing home facilities in the State of Michigan can elect to participate in Medicaid provided they are licensed and certified to do so.
- The total number of private nursing home facilities in the State of Michigan, including skilled nursing facilities and intermediate-care facilities, is approximately 450.
- The percentage of this total number of private nursing home facilities in the State of Michigan participating in Medicaid is approximately 85 percent.
- The current occupancy rate for private nursing home facilities in the State of Michigan is approximately 94 percent. This number is a statewide average and varies slightly from facility to facility.
- The average rate for a private paying resident in a private nursing home facility in the State of Michigan is approximately $55 per diem, or approximately $20,075 annually. This rate may vary slightly, depending upon whether the facility is a skilled nursing care or intermediate nursing care facility.

In the State of Michigan, private paying residents in a private nursing home facility participating in Medicaid cannot be asked to leave or be transferred when their funds have been exhausted, provided they are applying for Medicaid.

For further information on nursing homes and Medicaid in the State of Michigan call (517) 334-7245 (or write to address given for Michigan in the Medicaid Section).

MINNESOTA

- All private nursing home facilities in the State of Minnesota can elect to participate in Medicaid provided they are licensed and certified to do so.
- The total number of private nursing home facilities in the State of Minnesota, including skilled nursing facilities and intermediate-care facilities, is approximately 376.

- The percentage of this total number of private nursing home facilities in the State of Minnesota participating in Medicaid is approximately 100 percent.
- The current occupancy rate for private nursing home facilities in the State of Minnesota is approximately 94 percent. This number is a statewide average and varies slightly from facility to facility.
- The average rate for a private paying resident in a private nursing home facility in the State of Minnesota is approximately $60 per diem, or approximately $21,900 annually. This rate may vary slightly, depending upon whether the facility is a skilled nursing care or intermediate nursing care facility.

In the State of Minnesota, private paying residents in a private nursing home facility participating in Medicaid cannot be asked to leave or be transferred when their funds have been exhausted, provided they are applying for Medicaid. Minnesota also has a program which allows financial assistance to people who need care at home. The requirements for this program are that the applicant must be eligible for Medicaid if placed in a nursing home within 180 days. This is actually a sister-program to Medicaid and an alternative to going into a nursing home.

For further information on nursing homes and Medicaid in the State of Minnesota call (612) 297-3209 (or write to address given for Minnesota in the Medicaid Section).

MISSISSIPPI

- All private nursing home facilities in the State of Mississippi can elect to participate in Medicaid provided they are licensed and certified to do so.
- The total number of private nursing home facilities in the State of Mississippi, including skilled nursing facilities and intermediate-care facilities, is approximately 135.
- The percentage of this total number of private nursing home facilities in the State of Mississippi participating in Medicaid is approximately 82 percent.
- The current occupancy rate for private nursing home facilities in the State of Mississippi is approximately 96 percent.

This number is a statewide average and varies slightly from facility to facility.
- The average rate for a private paying resident in a private nursing home facility in the State of Mississippi is approximately $50 per diem, or approximately $18,250 annually. This rate may vary slightly, depending upon whether the facility is a skilled nursing care or intermediate nursing care facility.

In the State of Mississippi, private paying residents in a private nursing home facility participating in Medicaid cannot be asked to leave or be transferred when their funds have been exhausted, provided they are applying for Medicaid.

For further information on nursing homes and Medicaid in the State of Mississippi call (601) 359-6050 (or write to address given for Mississippi in the Medicaid Section).

MISSOURI

- All private nursing home facilities in the State of Missouri can elect to participate in Medicaid provided they are licensed and certified to do so.
- The total number of private nursing home facilities in the State of Missouri, including skilled nursing facilities and intermediate-care facilities, is approximately 605.
- The percentage of this total number of private nursing home facilities in the State of Missouri participating in Medicaid is approximately 58 percent.
- The current occupancy rate for private nursing home facilities in the State of Missouri is approximately 91 percent. This number is a statewide average and varies slightly from facility to facility.
- The average rate for a private paying resident in a private nursing home facility in the State of Missouri is approximately $60 per diem, or approximately $21,900 annually. This rate may vary slightly, depending upon whether the facility is a skilled nursing care or intermediate nursing care facility.

In the State of Missouri, private paying residents in a private nursing home facility participating in Medicaid cannot be asked to leave or be transferred when their funds have been exhausted, provided they are applying for Medicaid.

For further information on nursing homes and Medicaid in the State of Missouri call (314) 751-3401 (or write to address given for Missouri in the Medicaid Section).

MONTANA

- All private nursing home facilities in the State of Montana can elect to participate in Medicaid provided they are licensed and certified to do so.
- The total number of private nursing home facilities in the State of Montana, including skilled nursing facilities and intermediate-care facilities, is approximately 60.
- The percentage of this total number of private nursing home facilities in the State of Montana participating in Medicaid is approximately 100 percent.
- The current occupancy rate for private nursing home facilities in the State of Montana is approximately 92 percent. This number is a statewide average and varies slightly from facility to facility.
- The average rate for a private paying resident in a private nursing home facility in the State of Montana is approximately $54 per diem, or approximately $20,000 annually. This rate may vary slightly, depending upon whether the facility is a skilled nursing care or intermediate nursing care facility.

In the State of Montana, private paying residents in a private nursing home facility participating in Medicaid whose funds have been exhausted can be asked to leave for inability to pay, even though they have applied for Medicaid. This decision is left to the discretion of the individual facility.

For further information on nursing homes and Medicaid in the State of Montana call (404) 894-4859 (or write to address given for Montana in the Medicaid Section).

LONG-TERM HEALTH CARE FACILITIES

NEBRASKA

- All private nursing home facilities in the State of Nebraska can elect to participate in Medicaid provided they are licensed and certified to do so.
- The total number of private nursing home facilities in the State of Nebraska, including skilled nursing facilities and intermediate-care facilities, is approximately 168.
- The percentage of this total number of private nursing home facilities in the State of Nebraska participating in Medicaid is approximately 50 percent.
- The current occupancy rate for private nursing home facilities in the State of Nebraska is approximately 85 percent. This number is a statewide average and varies slightly from facility to facility.
- The average rate for a private paying resident in a private nursing home facility in the State of Nebraska is approximately $50 per diem, or approximately $21,900 annually. This rate may vary slightly, depending upon whether the facility is a skilled nursing care or intermediate nursing care facility.

A private paying resident in a private nursing home facility in the State of Nebraska participating in Medicaid must be a resident in the nursing home at least one year before applying for Medicaid.

However, if the number of residents on Medicaid in the nursing home is 10 percent or less than the total number of residents in the facility, then the individual who has exhausted his or her funds cannot be evicted because of an inability to pay or the nursing home will risk losing its license.

For further information on nursing homes and Medicaid in the State of Nebraska call (402) 471-3121 (or write to address given for Nebraska in the Medicaid Section).

NEVADA

- All private nursing home facilities in the State of Nevada can elect to participate in Medicaid provided they are licensed and certified to do so.

SURVIVING THE NOT SO GOLDEN YEARS

- The total number of private nursing home facilities in the State of Nevada, including skilled nursing facilities and intermediate-care facilities, is approximately 26.
- The percentage of this total number of private nursing home facilities in the State of Nevada participating in Medicaid is approximately 64 percent.
- The current occupancy rate for private nursing home facilities in the State of Nevada is approximately 98 percent. This number is a statewide average and varies slightly from facility to facility.
- The average rate for a private paying resident in a private nursing home facility in the State of Nevada is approximately $80 per diem, or approximately $28,800 annually. This rate may vary slightly, depending upon whether the facility is a skilled nursing care or intermediate nursing care facility.

In the State of Nevada, private paying residents in a private nursing home facility participating in Medicaid can be asked to leave or be transferred when their funds have been exhausted, even though they have applied for Medicaid. This decision is left to the discretion of the individual facility.

In the State of Nevada, sometimes the following practice is employed to circumvent the rules requiring that Medicaid patients be maintained: A private nursing home facility will accept a Medicaid patient and then fabricate some medical crisis necessitating that the Medicaid patient go to a hospital emergency room for 24 hours. While the Medicaid patient is in the emergency room, his or her bed is considered available and so the nursing home accepts a private paying patient in the place of the Medicaid patient. When the time comes for the Medicaid patient to return from the emergency room to the nursing home, his or her bed is no longer available and the Medicaid patient has nowhere to go.

Currently, this practice of sending Medicaid patients to hospital emergency rooms with alleged medical crises for the purpose of freeing up beds in the nursing home facilities for private paying patients has been greatly reduced. This is due to the adoption of certain policies by some hospitals requiring a 24-hour delay before admitting a nursing home resident for treatment, unless it is an obvious medical emergency.

LONG-TERM HEALTH CARE FACILITIES

During the course of researching this book, particularly the information on nursing home facilities, some horror stories were brought to my attention. One, as told to me by the former Deputy Administrator of Welfare—Director for Medicaid, for the state of Nevada, deserves repeating.

An 82-year-old woman, who although diabetic was in relatively good health, had to go to the hospital for moderate burns suffered on her extremities due to bathing in water which was too hot. After a brief stay in the hospital, during which time her burns healed, she was considered in good enough health to be released. However, the discharge staff decided that, due to her age and the fact that she lived alone, it would be in her best interest to place her in a nursing home facility. Within approximately 40 days after being admitted to the nursing home facility, this woman who had been in relative good health when admitted, was dead. She died from grave neglect. She had suffered through numerous incidents of seriously flawed health care delivery.

The current status of this particular case is that of being strongly considered for presentation to the state's Attorney General's Office on charges of adult neglect.

For further information on nursing homes and Medicaid in the State of Nevada call (702) 885-4698 (or write to address given for Nevada in the Medicaid Section).

NEW HAMPSHIRE

- All private nursing home facilities in the State of New Hampshire can elect to participate in Medicaid provided they are licensed and certified to do so.
- The total number of private nursing home facilities in the State of New Hampshire, including skilled nursing facilities and intermediate-care facilities, is approximately 62.
- The percentage of this total number of private nursing home facilities in the State of New Hampshire participating in Medicaid is approximately 93 percent.

- The current occupancy rate for private nursing home facilities in the State of New Hampshire is approximately 94 percent. This number is a statewide average and varies slightly from facility to facility.
- The average rate for a private paying resident in a private nursing home facility in the State of New Hampshire is approximately $82 per diem, or approximately $29,930 annually. This rate may vary slightly, depending upon whether the facility is a skilled nursing care or intermediate nursing care facility.

In the State of New Hampshire, private paying residents in a private nursing home facility participating in Medicaid cannot be asked to leave or be transferred when their funds have been exhausted, provided they are applying for Medicaid.

There is also a pre-screening program where a private paying resident is qualified as to eligibility for Medicaid both financially and medically but still is required to pay the nursing home for six months prior to applying for Medicaid.

For further information on nursing homes and Medicaid in the State of New Hampshire call (603) 271-4350 (or write to address given for New Hampshire in the Medicaid Section).

NEW JERSEY

- All private nursing home facilities in the State of New Jersey can elect to participate in Medicaid provided they are licensed and certified to do so.
- The total number of private nursing home facilities in the State of New Jersey, including skilled nursing facilities and intermediate-care facilities, is approximately 225.
- The percentage of this total number of private nursing home facilities in the State of New Jersey participating in Medicaid is approximately 60 percent.
- The current occupancy rate for private nursing home facilities in the State of New Jersey is approximately 90 percent. This number is a statewide average and varies slightly from facility to facility.

LONG-TERM HEALTH CARE FACILITIES

- The average rate for a private paying resident in a private nursing home facility in the State of New Jersey is approximately $85 per diem, or approximately $31,025 annually. This rate may vary slightly, depending upon whether the facility is a skilled nursing care or intermediate nursing care facility.

In the State of New Jersey, private paying residents in a private nursing home facility participating in Medicaid cannot be asked to leave or be transferred when their funds have been exhausted, provided they are applying for Medicaid.

For further information on nursing homes and Medicaid in the State of New Jersey call (609) 588-2600 (or write to address given for New Jersey in the Medicaid Section).

NEW MEXICO

- All private nursing home facilities in the State of New Mexico can elect to participate in Medicaid provided they are licensed and certified to do so.
- The total number of private nursing home facilities in the State of New Mexico, including skilled nursing facilities and intermediate-care facilities, is approximately 68.
- The percentage of this total number of private nursing home facilities in the State of New Mexico participating in Medicaid is approximately 90 percent.
- The current occupancy rate for private nursing home facilities in the State of New Mexico is approximately 93 percent. This number is a statewide average and varies slightly from facility to facility.
- The average rate for a private paying resident in a private nursing home facility in the State of New Mexico is approximately $100 per diem, or approximately $36,500 annually. This rate may vary slightly, depending upon whether the facility is a skilled nursing care or intermediate nursing care facility.

In the State of New Mexico, private paying residents in a private nursing home facility participating in Medicaid cannot be asked to leave or be transferred when their funds have been exhausted, provided they are applying for Medicaid.

For further information on nursing homes and Medicaid in the State of New Mexico call (505) 296-0021 (or write to address given for New Mexico in the Medicaid Section).

NEW YORK

- All private nursing home facilities in the State of New York can elect to participate in Medicaid provided they are licensed and certified to do so.
- The total number of private nursing home facilities in the State of New York, including skilled nursing facilities and intermediate-care facilities, is approximately 304.
- The percentage of this total number of private nursing home facilities in the State of New York participating in Medicaid is approximately 81 percent.
- The current occupancy rate for private nursing home facilities in the State of New York is approximately 99 percent. This number is a statewide average and varies slightly from facility to facility.
- The average rate for a private paying resident in a private nursing home facility in the State of New York is approximately $90 per diem, or approximately $32,850 annually. This rate may vary slightly, depending upon whether the facility is a skilled nursing care or intermediate nursing care facility.

In the State of New York, private paying residents in a private nursing home facility participating in Medicaid cannot be asked to leave or be transferred when their funds have been exhausted, provided they are applying for Medicaid.

For further information on nursing homes and Medicaid in the State of New York call (518) 473-5846 (or write to address given for New York in the Medicaid Section).

NORTH CAROLINA

- All private nursing home facilities in the State of North Carolina can elect to participate in Medicaid provided they are licensed and certified to do so.

LONG-TERM HEALTH CARE FACILITIES

- The total number of private nursing home facilities in the State of North Carolina, including skilled nursing facilities and intermediate-care facilities, is approximately 300.
- The percentage of this total number of private nursing home facilities in the State of North Carolina participating in Medicaid is approximately 85 percent.
- The current occupancy rate for private nursing home facilities in the State of North Carolina is approximately 90 percent. This number is a statewide average and varies slightly from facility to facility.
- The average rate for a private paying resident in a private nursing home facility in the State of North Carolina is approximately $70 per diem, or approximately $25,550 annually. This rate may vary slightly, depending upon whether the facility is a skilled nursing care or intermediate nursing care facility.

In the State of North Carolina, private paying residents in a private nursing home facility participating in Medicaid cannot be asked to leave or be transferred when their funds have been exhausted, provided they are applying for Medicaid.

For further information on nursing homes and Medicaid in the State of North Carolina call (919) 782-3827 (or write to address given for North Carolina in the Medicaid Section).

NORTH DAKOTA

- All private nursing home facilities in the State of North Dakota can elect to participate in Medicaid provided they are licensed and certified to do so.
- The total number of private nursing home facilities in the State of North Dakota, including skilled nursing facilities and intermediate-care facilities, is approximately 59.
- The percentage of this total number of private nursing home facilities in the State of North Dakota participating in Medicaid is approximately 56 percent.
- The current occupancy rate for private nursing home facilities in the State of North Dakota is approximately 96 percent. This number is a statewide average and varies slightly from facility to facility.

- The average rate for a private paying resident in a private nursing home facility in the State of North Dakota is approximately $53 per diem, or approximately $19,345 annually. This rate may vary slightly, depending upon whether the facility is a skilled nursing care or intermediate nursing care facility.

In the State of North Dakota, private paying residents in a private nursing home facility participating in Medicaid cannot be asked to leave or be transferred when their funds have been exhausted, provided they are applying for Medicaid.

For further information on nursing homes and Medicaid in the State of North Dakota call (701) 224-2177 (or write to address given for North Dakota in the Medicaid Section).

OHIO

- All private nursing home facilities in the State of Ohio can elect to participate in Medicaid provided they are licensed and certified to do so.
- The total number of private nursing home facilities in the State of Ohio, including skilled nursing facilities and intermediate-care facilities, is approximately 933.
- The percentage of this total number of private nursing home facilities in the State of Ohio participating in Medicaid is approximately 93 percent.
- The current occupancy rate for private nursing home facilities in the State of Ohio is approximately 91 percent. This number is a statewide average and varies slightly from facility to facility.
- The average rate for a private paying resident in a private nursing home facility in the State of Ohio is approximately $50 per diem, or approximately $18,250 annually. This rate may vary slightly, depending upon whether the facility is a skilled nursing care or intermediate nursing care facility.

LONG-TERM HEALTH CARE FACILITIES

In the State of Ohio, private paying residents in a private nursing home[4] facility participating in Medicaid cannot be asked to leave or be transferred when their funds have been exhausted, provided they are applying for Medicaid.

For further information on nursing homes and Medicaid in the State of Ohio call (614) 466-9243 (or write to address given for Ohio in the Medicaid Section).

OREGON

- All private nursing home facilities in the State of Oregon can elect to participate in Medicaid provided they are licensed and certified to do so.
- The total number of private nursing home facilities in the State of Oregon, including skilled nursing facilities and intermediate-care facilities, is approximately 175.
- The percentage of this total number of private nursing home facilities in the State of Oregon participating in Medicaid is approximately 95 percent.
- The current occupancy rate for private nursing home facilities in the State of Oregon is approximately 87 percent. This number is a statewide average and varies slightly from facility to facility.
- The average rate for a private paying resident in a private nursing home facility in the State of Oregon is approximately $60 per diem, or approximately $21,900 annually. This rate may vary slightly, depending upon whether the facility is a skilled nursing care or intermediate nursing care facility.

In the State of Oregon, private paying residents in a private nursing home facility participating in Medicaid cannot be asked to leave or be transferred when their funds have been exhausted, provided they are applying for Medicaid.

---

[4]For any problems regarding nursing homes the toll-free number is (800) 282-1206

For further information on nursing homes and Medicaid in the State of Oregon call (503) 378-3751 (or write to address given for Oregon in the Medicaid Section).

PENNSYLVANIA

- All private nursing home facilities in the State of Pennsylvania can elect to participate in Medicaid provided they are licensed and certified to do so.
- The total number of private nursing home facilities in the State of Pennsylvania, including skilled nursing facilities and intermediate-care facilities, is approximately 684.
- The percentage of this total number of private nursing home facilities in the State of Pennsylvania participating in Medicaid is approximately 89 percent.
- The current occupancy rate for private nursing home facilities in the State of Pennsylvania is approximately 95 percent. This number is a statewide average and varies slightly from facility to facility.
- The average rate for a private paying resident in a private nursing home facility in the State of Pennsylvania is approximately $88 per diem, or approximately $32,120 annually. This rate may vary slightly, depending upon whether the facility is a skilled nursing care or intermediate nursing care facility.

In the State of Pennsylvania, private paying residents in a private nursing home facility participating in Medicaid cannot be asked to leave or be transferred when their funds have been exhausted, provided they are applying for Medicaid.

For further information on nursing homes and Medicaid in the State of Pennsylvania call (215) 884-6776 (or write to address given for Pennsylvania in the Medicaid Section).

RHODE ISLAND

- All private nursing home facilities in the State of Rhode Island can elect to participate in Medicaid provided they are licensed and certified to do so.

LONG-TERM HEALTH CARE FACILITIES

- The total number of private nursing home facilities in the State of Rhode Island, including skilled nursing facilities and intermediate-care facilities, is approximately 120.
- The percentage of this total number of private nursing home facilities in the State of Rhode Island participating in Medicaid is approximately 72 percent.
- The current occupancy rate for private nursing home facilities in the State of Rhode Island is approximately 98 percent. This number is a statewide average and varies slightly from facility to facility.
- The average rate for a private paying resident in a private nursing home facility in the State of Rhode Island is approximately $86 per diem, or approximately $31,390 annually. This rate may vary slightly, depending upon whether the facility is a skilled nursing care or intermediate nursing care facility.

In the State of Rhode Island, private paying residents in a private nursing home facility participating in Medicaid cannot be asked to leave or be transferred when their funds have been exhausted, provided they are applying for Medicaid.

For further information on nursing homes and Medicaid in the State of Rhode Island call (401) 464-3575 (or write to address given for Rhode Island in the Medicaid Section).

SOUTH CAROLINA

- All private nursing home facilities in the State of South Carolina can elect to participate in Medicaid provided they are licensed and certified to do so.
- The total number of private nursing home facilities in the State of South Carolina, including skilled nursing facilities and intermediate-care facilities, is approximately 122.
- The percentage of this total number of private nursing home facilities in the State of South Carolina participating in Medicaid is approximately 90 percent.
- The current occupancy rate for private nursing home facilities in the State of South Carolina is approximately 97 percent. This number is a statewide average and varies slightly from facility to facility.

- The average rate for a private paying resident in a private nursing home facility in the State of South Carolina is approximately $60 per diem, or approximately $21,900 annually. This rate may vary slightly, depending upon whether the facility is a skilled nursing care or intermediate nursing care facility.

In the State of South Carolina, private paying residents in a private nursing home facility participating in Medicaid can be asked to leave or be transferred when their funds have been exhausted, even though they have applied for Medicaid. This decision is left to the discretion of the individual facility.

For further information on nursing homes and Medicaid in the State of South Carolina call (803) 253-6195 (or write to address given for South Carolina in the Medicaid Section).

SOUTH DAKOTA

- All private nursing home facilities in the State of South Dakota can elect to participate in Medicaid provided they are licensed and certified to do so.
- The total number of private nursing home facilities in the State of South Dakota, including skilled nursing facilities and intermediate-care facilities, is approximately 117.
- The percentage of this total number of private nursing home facilities in the State of South Dakota participating in Medicaid is approximately 97 percent.
- The current occupancy rate for private nursing home facilities in the State of South Dakota is approximately 97 percent. This number is a statewide average and varies slightly from facility to facility.
- The average rate for a private paying resident in a private nursing home facility in the State of South Dakota is approximately $47 per diem, or approximately $16,995 annually. This rate may vary slightly, depending upon whether the facility is a skilled nursing care or intermediate nursing care facility.

In the State of South Dakota, private paying residents in a private nursing home facility participating in Medicaid cannot

LONG-TERM HEALTH CARE FACILITIES

be asked to leave or be transferred when their funds have become exhausted, provided they are applying for Medicaid.

For further information on nursing homes and Medicaid in the State of South Dakota call (605) 773-3643 (or write to address given for South Dakota in the Medicaid Section).

TENNESSEE

● All private nursing home facilities in the State of Tennessee can elect to participate in Medicaid provided they are licensed and certified to do so.
● The total number of private nursing home facilities in the State of Tennessee, including skilled nursing facilities and intermediate-care facilities, is approximately 289.
● The percentage of this total number of private nursing home facilities in the State of Tennessee participating in Medicaid is approximately 100 percent.
● The current occupancy rate for private nursing home facilities in the State of Tennessee is approximately 93 percent. This number is a statewide average and varies slightly from facility to facility.
● The average rate for a private paying resident in a private nursing home facility in the State of Tennessee is approximately $60 per diem, or approximately $21,900 annually. This rate may vary slightly, depending upon whether the facility is a skilled nursing care or intermediate nursing care facility.

In the State of Tennessee, private paying residents in a private nursing home facility[5] participating in Medicaid cannot be asked to leave or be transferred when their funds have been exhausted, provided they are applying for Medicaid.

For further information on nursing homes and Medicaid in the State of Tennessee call (615) 741-0213 (or write to address given for Tennessee in the Medicaid Section).

---

[5]For any nursing home problems the toll-free number is (800) 523-2863.

SURVIVING THE NOT SO GOLDEN YEARS

TEXAS

- All private nursing home facilities in the State of Texas can elect to participate in Medicaid provided they are licensed and certified to do so.
- The total number of private nursing home facilities in the State of Texas, including skilled nursing facilities and intermediate-care facilities, is approximately 1,100.
- The percentage of this total number of private nursing home facilities in the State of Texas participating in Medicaid is approximately 95 percent.
- The current occupancy rate for private nursing home facilities in the State of Texas is approximately 80 percent. This number is a statewide average and varies slightly from facility to facility.
- The average rate for a private paying resident in a private nursing home facility in the State of Texas is approximately $50 per diem, or approximately $18,250 annually. This rate may vary slightly, depending upon whether the facility is a skilled nursing care or intermediate nursing care facility.

In the State of Texas, private paying residents in a private nursing home facility participating in Medicaid whose funds have been exhausted can be asked to leave for inability to pay even though they have applied for Medicaid. This decision is left to the discretion of the individual facility.

For further information on nursing homes and Medicaid in the State of Texas call (512) 450-7474 (or write to address given for Texas in the Medicaid Section).

UTAH

- All private nursing home facilities in the State of Utah can elect to participate in Medicaid provided they are licensed and certified to do so.
- The total number of private nursing home facilities in the State of Utah, including skilled nursing facilities and intermediate-care facilities, is approximately 87.

LONG-TERM HEALTH CARE FACILITIES

- The percentage of this total number of private nursing home facilities in the State of Utah participating in Medicaid is approximately 100 percent.
- The current occupancy rate for private nursing home facilities in the State of Utah is approximately 77 percent. This number is a statewide average and varies slightly from facility to facility.
- The average rate for a private paying resident in a private nursing home facility in the State of Utah is approximately $50 per diem, or approximately $18,250 annually. This rate may vary slightly, depending upon whether the facility is a skilled nursing care or intermediate nursing care facility.

In the State of Utah, private paying residents in a private nursing home facility participating in Medicaid cannot be asked to leave or be transferred when their funds have been exhausted, provided they are applying for Medicaid.

For further information on nursing homes and Medicaid in the State of Utah call (801) 538-6157 (or write to address given for Utah in the Medicaid Section).

VERMONT

- All private nursing home facilities in the State of Vermont can elect to participate in Medicaid provided they are licensed and certified to do so.
- The total number of private nursing home facilities in the State of Vermont, including skilled nursing facilities and intermediate-care facilities, is approximately 45.
- The percentage of this total number of private nursing home facilities in the State of Vermont participating in Medicaid is approximately 70 percent.
- The current occupancy rate for private nursing home facilities in the State of Vermont is approximately 98 percent. This number is a statewide average and varies slightly from facility to facility.
- The average rate for a private paying resident in a private nursing home facility in the State of Vermont is approximately $62 per diem, or approximately $22,630 annually. This rate may

vary slightly, depending upon whether the facility is a skilled nursing care or intermediate nursing care facility.

In the State of Vermont, private paying residents in a private nursing home facility participating in Medicaid cannot be asked to leave or be transferred when their funds have been exhausted, provided they are applying for Medicaid.

For further information on nursing homes and Medicaid in the State of Vermont call (802) 241-2880 (or write to address given for Vermont in the Medicaid Section).

VIRGINIA

- All private nursing home facilities in the State of Virginia can elect to participate in Medicaid provided they are licensed and certified to do so.
- The total number of private nursing home facilities in the State of Virginia, including skilled nursing facilities and intermediate-care facilities, is approximately 176.
- The percentage of this total number of private nursing home facilities in the State of Virginia participating in Medicaid is approximately 93 percent.
- The current occupancy rate for private nursing home facilities in the State of Virginia is approximately 95 percent. This number is a statewide average and varies slightly from facility to facility.
- The average rate for a private paying resident in a private nursing home facility in the State of Virginia is approximately $66 per diem, or approximately $24,000 annually. This rate may vary slightly, depending upon whether the facility is a skilled nursing care or intermediate nursing care facility.

In the State of Virginia, private paying residents in a private nursing home facility participating in Medicaid whose funds have been exhausted can be asked to leave for inability to pay even though they have applied for Medicaid. This decision is left to the discretion of the individual facility.

LONG-TERM HEALTH CARE FACILITIES

For further information on nursing homes and Medicaid in the State of Virginia call (804) 786-2082 (or write to address given for Virginia in the Medicaid Section).

WASHINGTON

- All private nursing home facilities in the State of Washington can elect to participate in Medicaid provided they are licensed and certified to do so.
- The total number of private nursing home facilities in the State of Washington, including skilled nursing facilities and intermediate-care facilities, is approximately 277.
- The percentage of this total number of private nursing home facilities in the State of Washington participating in Medicaid is approximately 65 percent.
- The current occupancy rate for private nursing home facilities in the State of Washington is approximately 95 percent. This number is a statewide average and varies slightly from facility to facility.
- The average rate for a private paying resident in a private nursing home facility in the State of Washington is approximately $60 per diem, or approximately $21,900 annually. This rate may vary slightly, depending upon whether the facility is a skilled nursing care or intermediate nursing care facility.

In the State of Washington, private paying residents in a private nursing home facility participating in Medicaid cannot be asked to leave or be transferred when their funds have been exhausted, provided they are applying for Medicaid.

For further information on nursing homes and Medicaid in the State of Washington call (206) 753-7313 (or write to address given for Washington in the Medicaid Section).

WEST VIRGINIA

- All private nursing home facilities in the State of West Virginia can elect to participate in Medicaid provided they are licensed and certified to do so.

- The total number of private nursing home facilities in the State of West Virginia, including skilled nursing facilities and intermediate-care facilities, is approximately 115.
- The percentage of this total number of private nursing home facilities in the State of West Virginia participating in Medicaid is approximately 70 percent.
- The current occupancy rate for private nursing home facilities in the State of West Virginia is approximately 94 percent. This number is a statewide average and varies slightly from facility to facility.
- The average rate for a private paying resident in a private nursing home facility in the State of West Virginia is approximately $60 per diem, or approximately $21,900 annually. This rate may vary slightly, depending upon whether the facility is a skilled nursing care or intermediate nursing care facility.

In the State of West Virginia, private paying residents in a private nursing home facility participating in Medicaid cannot be asked to leave or be transferred when their funds have been exhausted, provided they are applying for Medicaid.

For further information on nursing homes and Medicaid in the State of West Virginia call (304) 348-8990 (or write to address given for West Virginia in the Medicaid Section).

WISCONSIN

- All private nursing home facilities in the State of Wisconsin can elect to participate in Medicaid provided they are licensed and certified to do so.
- The total number of private nursing home facilities in the State of Wisconsin, including skilled nursing facilities and intermediate-care facilities, is approximately 22.
- The percentage of this total number of private nursing home facilities in the State of Wisconsin participating in Medicaid is approximately 97 percent.
- The current occupancy rate for private nursing home facilities in the State of Wisconsin is approximately 93 percent. This number is a statewide average and varies slightly from facility to facility.

LONG-TERM HEALTH CARE FACILITIES

● The average rate for a private paying resident in a private nursing home facility in the State of Wisconsin is approximately $80 per diem, or approximately $29,200 annually. This rate may vary slightly, depending upon whether the facility is a skilled nursing care or intermediate nursing care facility.

In the State of Wisconsin, private paying residents in a private nursing home facility participating in Medicaid cannot be asked to leave or be transferred when their funds have been exhausted, provided they are applying for Medicaid.

For further information on nursing homes and Medicaid in the State of Wisconsin call (608) 267-9591 (or write to address given for Wisconsin in the Medicaid Section).

WYOMING

● All private nursing home facilities in the State of Wyoming can elect to participate in Medicaid provided they are licensed and certified to do so.
● The total number of private nursing home facilities in the State of Wyoming, including skilled nursing facilities and intermediate-care facilities, is approximately 29.
● The percentage of this total number of private nursing home facilities in the State of Wyoming participating in Medicaid is approximately 100 percent.
● The current occupancy rate for private nursing home facilities in the State of Wyoming is approximately 90 percent. This number is a statewide average and varies slightly from facility to facility.
● The average rate for a private paying resident in a private nursing home facility in the State of Wyoming is approximately $70 per diem, or approximately $25,550 annually. This rate may vary slightly, depending upon whether the facility is a skilled nursing care or intermediate nursing care facility.

In the State of Wyoming, private paying residents in a private nursing home facility participating in Medicaid cannot be asked to leave or be transferred when their funds have been exhausted, provided they are applying for Medicaid.

SURVIVING THE NOT SO GOLDEN YEARS

For further information on nursing homes and Medicaid in the State of Wyoming call (307) 777-7121 (or write to address given for Wyoming in the Medicaid Section).

Chapter 7

OTHER OPTIONS

"I DIDN'T KNOW HELP WAS AVAILABLE"

How often has someone you know uttered the above statement? Or how often has someone thought it, after having survived some seemingly endless crisis.

Ignorance! Ignorance is our own worst enemy. In this country presently, we are changing our diets, controlling cholesterol and fat intake to fight heart disease, and lowering the mortality rate from heart attacks. We have launched a major campaign against smoking, due to the inherent health hazards in the habit. Hopefully, by doing this, we are positively impacting the mortality rate from lung cancer. We are seriously involved in a national war on drugs and once again our main artillery is an arsenal of facts and information on the subject matter. Through these efforts we are educating people and raising their consciousness on these issues. We are teaching them and helping them to understand that through knowledge they can fight back. They can change the situation.

The same principle applies to health care issues and in particular, long-term health care. Primarily we can't help ourselves and others if we are ignorant of the facts or if we don't know what is available to us. Overwhelming helplessness and financial bankruptcy in the face of major long-term health care problems are not always the only alternatives. There are other options. But we need to know what they are.

In essence, assistance is available and it comes to us in the form of federal programs such as Medicaid and Medicare. In previous chapters some of the options under Medicaid have been discussed. These are some of the options and services available to us under Medicare. The Medicare Program is a two-part coverage: Hospital Insurance and Medical Insurance. Generally you are automatically eligible for Part A—Hospital Insurance if:

- you are 65 or over and entitled to monthly Social Security or Railroad Retirement
- you have worked long enough to be insured under Social Security or the Railroad Retirement system
- you would be entitled to monthly Social Security benefits based on the work record of your spouse and your spouse is at least 62 (you spouse need not apply for benefits)
- you have worked long enough in federal, state, or local government employment to be insured for Medicare purposes

Part B—Medical Insurance (the voluntary portion of Medicare) covers physicians' services; hospital out-patient services and supplies such as diagnostic x-rays or x-rays which are a part of treatment and therapy; out-patient physical therapy and speech pathology services; other medical services and health services such as surgical dressings, splints, and casts; rental and/or purchase of prosthetic devices and ambulance services.

Anyone considered eligible for Part A is generally eligible for Part B but must pay a monthly premium. That premium for the year 1990 is $28.60 per month. Both Medicare Part A and Part B cover some of the costs of Home Health Care administered by a certified public or private Home Health Care Agency. This may cover partial payment for intermittent part-time skilled care from registered nurses, therapists, and home health aides. Intermittent part-time care is generally considered to be day care for five days a week for up to two or three weeks.

LONG-TERM HEALTH CARE FACILITIES

To qualify for Home Health Care under Medicare a recipient must meet all of the following criteria:

- be homebound
- be under the care of a physician
- need care for specific illness
- need skilled services
- need services on a part-time basis

In addition, one may be eligible for skilled services such as nursing, physical or speech therapy, or for occupational therapy, social services, and home heath-aide services, as prescribed by your physician.

PRIOR HOSPITALIZATION IS NOT A PREREQUISITE FOR HOME HEALTH CARE SERVICES UNDER MEDICARE. Home Health Care can even be covered by Medicaid in some cases if the person who qualifies for admittance to a nursing home chooses Home Health Care as a viable alternative.

Other supportive services, such as adult day care centers, meal programs, and support groups, are available through the community.

All of these programs and perhaps more, are out there. We can't possibly be aware of all of them. Therefore, we must not hesitate to ask people who do know and who are in a position to help us. For example, we should not bring someone home from the hospital who will need continued care without asking the appropriate hospital personnel or social workers to help us make arrangements for this continued care. As in any situation involving care for the elderly, we should at least know whom to contact to find out the answers to our questions.

For questions relating to Medicare and what is available from Federal Programs, you should contact your local Social Security Office or call Medicare directly at (800) 234-5752. For questions on community-based services it would be appropriate to call your State Agency on Aging. They in turn can provide you with the telephone number of your Area Agency on Aging. It is important to bear in mind the fact that the mere existence of these programs will do us absolutely no good unless we use them.

SURVIVING THE NOT SO GOLDEN YEARS

The following is a list of State Agencies and their telephone numbers:

STATE AGENCY	TELEPHONE
Alabama Commission on Aging	(205) 261-5743
Older Alaskans Commission	(907) 564-3250
American Samoa Territorial Administration on Aging	(684) 633-1252
Arizona Office on Aging and Adult Administration	(602) 255-4446
Arkansas Department of Human Services	(501) 371-2441
California Department of Aging	(916) 322-5290
Colorado Aging & Adult Services Division	(303) 866-5122
Connecticut Department on Aging	(203) 566-3268
Delaware Division on Aging	(302) 421-6791
District of Columbia Office of Aging	(202) 724-5622
Florida Aging and Adult Services	(904) 488-8922
Georgia Office of Aging	(404) 894-5333
Guam Public Health and Social Services	(671) 734-2942
Hawaii Executive Office on Aging	(808) 548-2593
Idaho Office on Aging	(208) 334-3833

LONG-TERM HEALTH CARE FACILITIES

STATE AGENCY	TELEPHONE
Illinois Department on Aging	(217) 785-3356
Indiana Department on Aging and Community Services	(317) 232-7006
Iowa Community on Aging	(515) 281-5187
Kansas Department on Aging	(913) 296-4986
Kentucky Division for Aging Services	(502) 564-6930
Louisiana Governor's Office of Elderly Affairs	(504) 925-1700
Maine Bureau of Elderly	(207) 289-2561
Maryland Office on Aging	(301) 225-1102
Massachusetts Department of Elder Affairs	(617) 727-7751
Michigan Office of Services to the Aging	(517) 373-8230
Minnesota Board on Aging	(612) 296-2770
Mississippi Council on Aging	(601) 949-2013
Missouri Division of Aging	(314) 751-3082
Montana Community Services Division	(406) 444-3865
Nebraska Department on Aging	(402) 471-2307
Nevada Division for Aging Services	(702) 885-4210

SURVIVING THE NOT SO GOLDEN YEARS

STATE AGENCY	TELEPHONE
New Hampshire State Council on Aging	(603) 271-2751
New Jersey Division on Aging	(609) 292-4833
New Mexico State Agency on Aging	(505) 827-7640
New York State Office for the Aging	(518) 474-4425
North Carolina Division of Aging	(919) 733-3983
North Dakota Aging Services	(701) 224-2577
Northern Mariana Islands Department of Community and Cultural Affairs	(670) 234-6011
Ohio Commission on Aging	(614) 466-5500
Oklahoma Services for the Aging	(405) 521-2281
Oregon Senior Services Division	(503) 378-4728
Pennsylvania Department of Aging	(717) 783-1550
Puerto Rico Gericulture Commission	(809) 724-1059
Rhode Island Department of Elderly Affairs	(401) 277-2858
South Carolina Commission on Aging	(803) 758-2576
South Dakota Office of Adult Services and Aging	(605) 773-3656
Tennessee Commission on Aging	(615) 741-2056
Texas Department on Aging	(512) 444-6890

LONG-TERM HEALTH CARE FACILITIES

STATE AGENCY	TELEPHONE
Trust Territory of the Pacific Islands Office of Elderly Affairs	(670) 322-9328
Utah Division of Agency and Adult Services	(801) 533-6422
Vermont Office on Aging	(802) 241-2400
Virgin Islands Commission on Aging	(809) 774-5884
Virginia Department for the Aging	(804) 225-2271
Washington Bureau of Aging and Adult Services	(206) 753-2502
West Virginia Commission on Aging	(304) 348-3317
Wisconsin Office on Aging	(608) 266-2536
Wyoming Commission on Aging	(307) 777-6111

PART THREE

Financial Considerations

Chapter 8

PROTECTING YOUR ASSETS

FAMILY SITUATIONS THAT SHOULD FLAG POTENTIAL FINANCIAL PROBLEMS

There are numerous books on personal finances available in libraries and bookstores, all carefully prepared and written by experts in the field of economics and investment. Each of these experts is more than eager to tell you how to protect your assets and how to invest your finances for the security of your future. However, this book approaches the problem of financial security from a slightly different aspect—that of the person himself or herself, a spouse, a close relative, or a friend, single or married, who anticipates facing or is already facing the prospect of going into a long-term health care facility as a permanent resident. Some of these financial problems will be similar to those of the average person, but some problems will be unique, due to the circumstances. These people do not come from destitute or impoverished backgrounds. They are all basically middle-income people, ranging from lower to higher middle-income, but all facing a common crisis: the event of going into a long-term health care facility for the remainder of their lives, with the potential of totally wiping out any savings, funds, or assets they had put aside for their golden years. This is not even taking into consideration any calamitous illness that

SURVIVING THE NOT SO GOLDEN YEARS

may befall them. This is merely covering the annual costs of a long-term health care facility. Securing one's personal finances in the face of unexpected health care is a traumatic realization for people as they reach their older years and one that has devastated many lives, including those of immediate families.

BASIC STEPS FOR ASSESSING YOUR OWN OR SOMEONE ELSE'S FINANCIAL POSITION

There are, however, ways in which these devastating financial circumstances can be lessened to some degree or, in some instances, even avoided. To begin with, certain steps should be taken immediately to evaluate the person's finances and assets. Following is a sample inventory list which can be helpful in determining a person's total net worth:

Cash/Monetary Investments
- Cash on hand
- Checking account
- Savings account
- CDs (certificate of deposit)
- Treasury notes
- Bonds (corporate, Treasury, municipal, convertible)
- Mutual funds
- Stocks
- IRAs

Business and Real Estate
- Business partnerships (limited or otherwise)
- Real estate property (investment, rental)

Retirement Funds and Pensions
- Civil Service
- Foreign Service
- Military service
- Railroad retirement
- Corporate pension plans
- Retirement plans (corporate)
- Keogh profit sharing plans
- Corporate profit sharing plans

FINANCIAL CONSIDERATIONS

Insurance
    Whole life
    Term
    Annuity
    Accident
    Other

Personal possessions
    Home
    Car
    Paintings
    Sculptures
    Artifacts
    Antiques
    Rare books
    Jewelry
    Silverware, china, crystal
    Other valuables

Against this list and its net worth you should list outstanding debts such as:

Mortgages (should there be any)
Auto loans
Credit card loans
Private or personal loans
Other

When you have added up the sum total of outstanding debts and subtracted them from the net-asset worth, you will have an approximate idea of this person's net worth in assets. This would have to be considered also in terms of whether a person is single or married, whether the assets are joint or belong exclusively to one spouse, and finally, how the state where this person resides treats these assets.

OPTIONS FOR SPENDING DOWN— SHOULD IT BE NECESSARY

This situation presumes a middle-income couple with some assets, where financial assistance may not be immediately necessary to cover the cost of the long-term health care facility. However, "spending down" may be necessary before applying for Medicaid. This is a process whereby a person's assets are reduced in order to meet Medicaid eligibility requirements. In most cases this can be accomplished by simply paying the cost of the nursing home facility or other outstanding medical expenses. Eventually, through this process, most individuals' assets dwindle to the point where they are at the level acceptable for Medicaid eligibility. This formula can also be applied where the individual's gross monthly income is in excess of the allowable level for Medicaid eligibility. The accumulation of medical expenses and other expenses related to health care, when deducted from the gross monthly income, usually reduces this figure to the acceptable level for Medicaid eligibility.

Other factors to be considered when determining what might be allowable as legitimate deductible expenses from the assets of a Medicaid applicant are expenses incurred in trying to locate a suitable nursing home facility for an immediate family member, particularly if he or she is out of state.

Example: A married daughter and her family reside in one part of the country and her parents in another. One of the parents becomes seriously ill and must be placed in a skilled nursing home. The other parent is terribly devastated and barely able to care for himself. This situation causes great concern for the daughter—having both her parents so far away under these circumstances is really not feasible or acceptable. Some legitimate expenses will have to be incurred in relocating the parents to an area closer to the daughter where there is also a suitable nursing home facility.

In some states, when these expenses are reasonably necessary and substantiated by thorough documentation—bills, receipts, etc.—they can be considered legitimate deductions from the assets of the would-be Medicaid applicant. However, any doubts as to the legitimacy of incurred expenses on behalf

FINANCIAL CONSIDERATIONS

of the Medicaid applicant, as have been discussed above, should be addressed to the local Medicaid office, as such interpretations and allowances vary from state to state.

WHY AND WHEN TO SEEK PROFESSIONAL ADVICE IN PLANNING YOUR FINANCIAL ASSETS PROTECTION

Previously this book has discussed some very simple methods of assessing the finances of someone who faces the possibility of going into a long-term health care facility. Now we will briefly examine why this needs to be done. The crisis of having to go into a long-term health care facility permanently is usually a critical time for a family, both financially and emotionally. The overwhelming costs of a skilled or intermediate-care facility are enough to financially traumatize the most stable of families. The idea that practically all of a couple's life savings and assets, save for their home and some basic exemptions, as previously discussed, will go to cover basic long-term health care costs, is shattering. To many who have worked all their lives, this was to be their time to enjoy together. Now, not only must they endure the silent grief of this tragic separation and in some cases, as with Alzheimer's, watch helplessly as their partner suffers a living death, but they must also watch all their resources being drained to maintain the necessary level of health care needed for this person.

All these grim facts and experiences staring us in the face should awaken us to the hope that some prudent financial planning in advance can perhaps prevent economic disaster for all concerned.

Primarily there are some very basic steps that should be investigated:

Power of Attorney. This is a written document granting another person the ability to act in your (his/her) behalf for certain stated purposes as long as you (he/she) remain mentally competent.

Durable Power of Attorney. This is basically the same as above, only it prevails even if you (he/she) should become mentally incompetent.

Trust. There are myriad trusts, any one of which may be suitable to your needs and financially advantageous to have established. Basically, a trust involves drawing up a legal document, turning over certain assets to someone else's charge (trustee) to hold and manage for the benefit of a third party (the beneficiary).

Guardianship. This is another legal step that should be considered as a person's mental faculties start to fail. Guardianships are regulated by the state and there are several kinds: voluntary, involuntary, temporary, permanent, limited, or total. Basically, guardianship in the case of the elderly with impaired mental awareness is where the court finds the person, based on competent medical testimony, incapable of functioning in a decision-making capacity. Therefore, power to act on this person's behalf is then transferred legally to a responsible adult who then becomes the guardian. This can be beneficial in that it prevents the person of failing mental faculties from legitimately signing any legal documents which could be detrimental to him- or herself as well as to loved ones, such as signing documents giving away assets or money, signing documents for unnecessary surgery, or even signing a will that has been falsified.

Will. This is a way of administering or disposing of your (his/her) estate (personal effects—all possessions, properties, etc., anything that is yours/his/hers) after death and insuring that these wishes will be implemented according to your/his/her specifications. It must be a written document that will physically survive after the person's death. It must comply totally with the state law and must be witnessed by two or three competent adults, depending on the state's laws. A will is also one of the few legal and effective tools generally used to avoid the probate of one's estate.

FINANCIAL CONSIDERATIONS

Living Will.[1] This is available in only a very few states. It is a very delicate issue because of the nature of its content. Basically, it is a legal document which states that if a person's physical condition is grave enough so that his or her only means of existing (as certified by two competent physicians) is through the continued use of *extraordinary means* of life support systems, this person will have declared, by virtue of having signed this document, a wish not to have their life extended through these measures. In the case of a person who is legally considered mentally incompetent, his/her legal guardian may assume the responsibility of signing this document.

Transfer of assets. This was covered previously in the section on Medicaid. However, it is a topic which should be included among issues to be raised in discussions with your attorney or advisor. In the instance where there is a strong likelihood of a family member having to go into a long-term health care facility permanently and at some point having to apply for Medicaid, it would be prudent to discuss the advisability of transferring some or all of this person's assets to another family member. This could apply specifically in the case of a family heirloom or a personal possession which is not only of great financial value but also of great sentimental value. Currently it is perfectly legal to transfer any or all assets of any person applying for Medicaid, providing that the transfer is completed 30 months prior to making application for Medicaid.

One consideration that is probably of utmost concern to anyone dealing with all these numerous problems and questions as to the future financial security as well as the reas-

---

[1] A living will, by its very nature, is a very controversial and weighty issue and above all an extremely serious decision for anyone to make. The above paragraph is by no means an in-depth or comprehensive definition of the subject. Therefore, before exercising the option of signing a "living will," be certain that the person involved has been thoroughly counselled and is completely aware of all the facts and ramifications involved in this decision.

surances of good health care of their loved one should be where and how is the best way to safeguard the finances and assets of this person. We may feel tempted, because we consider ourselves well informed, to do it ourselves. However, it could happen that despite how much we think we know, through ignorance or by overlooking one tiny detail, the end result could be a deadly, irrevocable, and costly mistake, with devastating consequences that we would regret, with the added frustration that there was no one to blame but ourselves. The best answer to this question is to obtain professional advice, either from a competent qualified attorney or a qualified financial advisor.

ISSUES TO RAISE IN ORDER TO DETERMINE THE QUALIFICATIONS OF THE PROFESSIONAL YOU CHOOSE

The next logical thought along these lines is how to find an attorney and subsequently how to reassure ourselves that he or she is best qualified to handle our needs.

Initially, bear in mind that your current family lawyer who has handled your home-closings, who has helped with your tax questions, or has perhaps represented you in an accident suit, or even helped your closest friend with her or his divorce, is not necessarily qualified to handle your financial affairs. Nor should you feel obligated to consult with any relative just because he or she is a member of the family, even though a practicing corporate attorney. Handling your finances and determining what is best for you is a deadly serious matter and a responsibility you should be willing to share only with someone in whom you have implicit trust.

Where can you find an attorney of this caliber? You might start by calling your state's Bar Association and asking for an attorney referral in this field of specialization. You should inquire at your local university (law school division). You should inquire at organizations or associations who specialize in the field of financial planning. Ask friends and acquaintances who might have faced similar situations for referrals. Even ask lawyers, who should not be offended if this is not their area of expertise, for referrals. And finally check the yellow

FINANCIAL CONSIDERATIONS

pages. After all, before you decide you are going to interview and judge the qualifications of this person.

To begin with, after you have received the names of several attorneys who appear to be suited to handling your affairs, call and set up an appointment. Be sure to determine if there is an initial consultation fee and if so, what it is.

(1) Prepare in advance of your meeting a list of topics you might want to touch on to determine how well versed he or she is in these matters.
(2) Ask if he or she handles these kinds of cases on a regular basis or only occasionally.
(3) Ask for the names of some clients, for reference purposes.
(4) Ask the attorney if he or she will be personally handling your affairs and if not, who will.
(5) Ask for an approximate length of time necessary to prepare your financial affairs.

In conjunction with the above, ask for an estimate of what his or her services will cost you. Also ask if the fee is based on hourly services or is just a flat fee for the type of work. (It might be helpful if your attorney is familiar with the current laws for Medicaid eligibility, such as the transfer of assets and resources, etc.)

Finally, when you have selected someone whom you trust and who you feel is most capable of serving your best interests financially, advise him or her of the following:

- that you wish to participate to whatever extent is necessary in the developing of this financial strategy and you are willing to assist by furnishing all materials such as family papers, documents, etc., that would facilitate or expedite this procedure
- that you want to know how he or she proposes to help secure your (spouse's/parent's) financial future; that you wish to be kept informed at all times of all progress and any developments with the formation of this plan
- last, that you want to strongly reaffirm to your attorney or advisor your faith in his or her ability to meet and serve your best interests, but commensurately you would like them to

understand and respect your strong and justifiable sense of responsibility and desire for participation in the development of this strategy as, in the final analysis, it is you who will have to live with this plan

PART FOUR

Directory of Government Representatives

Chapter 9

YOU *CAN* MAKE A DIFFERENCE

In the previous sections we have provided some of the current basic regulations for Medicaid, under the Aged Category, in each of the 50 states, as well as some of the differences in the laws governing nursing homes participating in Medicaid in each of the 50 states. If these laws seem inequitable from state to state, or in a particular state appear inadequate, and you feel they should be changed, communicate this to your federal and state representatives.

Congress, as well as all government officials, work for you. Their salaries are paid by your tax dollars. They are your voice in the government and in determining the laws by which we live. If these laws don't seem fair to you, then it is up to you to change them.

Following are the lists of telephone numbers and addresses of the local district offices of all the Governors, Senators, and Representatives for each state. In the U.S. capital (Washington, D.C.) any member of Congress (Senator or Representative) can be reached by calling (202) 224-3121 and asking the operator for the Senator or Representative by name.

When corresponding with the members of Congress, state legislators, assemblymen, or with any government official, the following suggestions are offered:

GUIDELINES FOR CORRESPONDING WITH GOVERNMENT OFFICIALS

(1) Identify yourself—stating that you are one of their constituents.
(2) State your reason or reasons for writing—personal and factual.
(3) Be brief—try to keep to one page.
(4) If you are requesting action—be specific and clear as to whether it is some action to be taken on a piece of legislation or whether you are seeking information.
(5) Include your return address in the heading of your letter–then people can respond to you if necessary.

Sample letters follow, on the next several pages. There are four—probably all of the types that you might need.

DIRECTORY OF GOVERNMENT REPRESENTATIVES

SAMPLES OF CORRESPONDENCE

Here are four samples of correspondence to these officials:

SAMPLE LETTER #1

1234 Any Street
Any City, State, 12345
Month/Day/Year

Congressman John Q. Public
Any Street
Any City, State, 12345

Dear Congressman Public:

My name is John Doe and I am an active member of your constituency.

In my opinion the rising costs of medical care in this country and the commensurate inability of many people to meet these costs either due to lack of private insurance (which many working people cannot afford) or because there is no National Health Care Program, is a cause of grave concern to me.

I would like to see a greater percentage of my tax dollar allocated toward the development of a National Health Care Program. Please advise me as to what I can do to help make this materialize.

Very truly yours,

John Doe

SURVIVING THE NOT SO GOLDEN YEARS

SAMPLE LETTER #2

1234 Any Street
Any City, State, 12345
Month/Day/Year

Governor John Q. Public
Any Street
Any City, State, 12345

Dear Governor Public:

Recently I have learned that the financial requirements for Medicaid eligibility for the aged are more stringent in our state than in most states. This poses undue hardship on those of us who need the benefits of Medicaid to cover our rising health care costs.

I would like to see our criteria liberalized to benefit and to cover more of the aged population who are in need of this financial assistance. I feel it is imperative that legislation be introduced to enact this.

Very truly yours,

Jane Doe

DIRECTORY OF GOVERNMENT REPRESENTATIVES

SAMPLE LETTER #3

```
1234 Any Street
Any City, State, 12345
Month/Day/Year

Governor John Q. Public
Any Street
Any City, State, 12345
```

Dear Governor Public:

It has come to my attention that in our state private paying patients in private nursing home facilities whose funds have been exhausted can be asked to leave, because of an inability to pay, even while applying for Medicaid. In most other states, private paying patients are protected by state law from being evicted because of an inability to pay.

This situation, as it exists in our state, is unconscionable and morally unacceptable.

I would like to see legislation enacted in our state, comparable to the legislation existing in those states which legally protect these residents in nursing home facilities.

Very truly yours,

Jane Doe

SURVIVING THE NOT SO GOLDEN YEARS

SAMPLE LETTER #4

1234 Any Street
Any City, State, 12345
Month/Day/Year

Senator John Q. Public
Any Street
Any City, State, 12345

Dear Senator Public:

My name is Jane Doe and I am an active member of your constituency.

Recently, due to personal experience (illness of a parent or loved one) (working with the aged) (counselling, etc.), it has come to my attention the appalling lack of funds available to help mitigate the rising cost of health care for the elderly--a segment of our population that is on the increase.

Please, Senator Public, provide me with the following information:

(A) Currently, what is the percentage of my tax money being allocated for the Medicare and Medicaid programs?

(B) What is your position on our current health care programs and what has been your previous voting record on the following issues: Medicaid, Medicare, the Catastrophic Health Bill, and Social Security?

(C) Have you any plans to introduce new legislation which will expand the provisions and financial allocations for these health care programs?

Very truly yours,

Jane Doe

DIRECTORY OF GOVERNMENT REPRESENTATIVES

NAMES, ADDRESSES, AND TELEPHONE
NUMBERS OF MEMBERS OF CONGRESS
AND OF GOVERNORS

ALABAMA

SENATORS	DISTRICT OFFICE	TEL. NO.
Howard Heflin	Montgomery, AL	205-832-7287
Richard Shelby	Tuscaloosa, AL	205-759-5047

REPRESENTATIVES	DISTRICT OFFICE	TEL. NO.
Sonny Callahan	Mobile, AL	205-690-2811
William Dickinson	Montgomery, AL	205-832-7292
Tom Bevill	Jasper, AL	205-221-2310
Ronnie G. Flippo	Huntsville, AL	205-772-0244
Claude Harris	Tuscaloosa, AL	205-752-3578
Glenn Browder	Anniston, AL	205-236-5655
Ben Erdreich	Birmingham, AL	205-731-0956

GOVERNOR	OFFICE	ADDRESS
Guy Hunt	State House	Montgomery, AL 36130
	RESIDENCE	ADDRESS
	Executive Mansion	Montgomery, AL 36104

ALASKA

SENATORS	DISTRICT OFFICE	TEL. NO.
Ted Stevens	Juneau, AK	907-586-7400
Frank H. Murkowski	Anchorage, AK	907-271-3735

REPRESENTATIVE	DISTRICT OFFICE	TEL. NO.
Don Young	Fairbanks, AK	907-456-0210

SURVIVING THE NOT SO GOLDEN YEARS

GOVERNOR	OFFICE	ADDRESS
Steve Cowper	P.O. Box A	Juneau, AK 99811
	RESIDENCE	ADDRESS
	Governor's House	Juneau, AK 99801

ARIZONA

SENATORS	DISTRICT OFFICE	TEL. NO.
Dennis DeConcini	Tucson, AZ	602-629-6831
John McCain	Phoenix, AZ	602-640-2567
REPRESENTATIVES	DISTRICT OFFICE	TEL. NO.
John J. Rhodes III	Mesa, AZ	602-831-6433
Morris K. Udall	Tucson, AZ	602-629-6404
Bob Stump	Phoenix, AZ	602-261-6923
Jon Kyl	Phoenix, AZ	602-840-1891
Jim Kolbe	Tucson, AZ	602-322-3555
GOVERNOR	OFFICE	ADDRESS
Rose Mofford	State House	Phoenix, AZ 85007
	RESIDENCE	ADDRESS
	330 West Maryland	Phoenix, AZ 85013

ARKANSAS

SENATORS	DISTRICT OFFICE	TEL. NO.
Dale Bumpers	Little Rock, AR	501-378-6286
David Pryor	Little Rock, AR	501-378-6336
REPRESENTATIVES	DISTRICT OFFICE	TEL. NO.
Bill Alexander	Jonesboro, AR	501-972-4600
Tommy F. Robinson	Little Rock, AR	501-378-5941

DIRECTORY OF GOVERNMENT REPRESENTATIVES

John Paul
    Hammerschmidt   Fort Smith, AR   501-782-7787
Beryl Anthony, Jr.   Hot Springs, AR   501-624-1011

GOVERNOR	OFFICE	ADDRESS
Bill Clinton	State Capitol	Little Rock, AR 72201
	RESIDENCE	ADDRESS
	Governor's Mansion	Little Rock, AR 72206

CALIFORNIA

SENATORS	DISTRICT OFFICE	TEL. NO.
Alan Cranston	Los Angeles, CA	213-215-2186
Pete Wilson	San Francisco, CA	415-556-4307

REPRESENTATIVES	DISTRICT OFFICE	TEL. NO.
Douglas Bosco	Santa Rosa, CA	707-525-4235
Wall Herger	Chico, CA	916-893-8363
Robert T. Matsui	Sacramento, CA	916-551-2846
Vic Fazio	Sacramento, CA	916-978-4381
Nancy Pelosi	San Francisco, CA	415-556-4862
Barbara Boxer	San Rafael, CA	415-457-7272
George Miller	Pleasant Hill, CA	415-687-3260
Ronald V. Dellums	Oakland, CA	415-763-0370
Fortney Pete Stark	Hayward, CA	415-635-1092
Don Edwards	San Jose, CA	408-247-1711
Tom Lantos	San Mateo, CA	415-342-0300
Tom Campbell	Sunnyvale, CA	408-245-4835
Norman Y. Mineta	San Jose, CA	408-984-6045
Norman D. Shumway	Stockton, CA	209-957-7773
Gary Condit	Modesto, CA	209-527-1914
Leon E. Panetta	Monterey, CA	408-649-3555
Charles Pashayan, Jr.	Fresno, CA	209-487-5500
Richard H. Lehman	Fresno, CA	209-487-5760

SURVIVING THE NOT SO GOLDEN YEARS

Robert J. Lagomarsino	Santa Barbara, CA	805-963-1708
William M. Thomas	Bakersfield, CA	805-327-3611
Elton Gallegly	Chatsworth, CA	818-341-2121
Carlos J. Moorhead	Pasadena, CA	818-792-6168
Anthony C. Beilenson	Los Angeles, CA	213-209-7801
Henry A. Waxman	Los Angeles, CA	213-651-1040
Edward R. Roybal	Los Angeles, CA	213-894-4870
Howard L. Berman	Panorama City, CA	818-891-0543
Mel Levine	Los Angeles, CA	213-410-9415
Julian C. Dixon	Inglewood, CA	213-678-5424
Augustus F. Hawkins	Los Angeles, CA	213-233-0733
Matthew M. Martinez	Montebello, CA	213-722-7731
Mervyn M. Dymally	Compton, CA	213-632-4318
Glenn M. Anderson	Long Beach, CA	213-437-7665
David Dreier	Covina, CA	818-339-9078
Esteban Edward Torres	Pico Rivera, CA	213-695-0702
Jerry Lewis	Redlands, CA	714-862-6030
George E. Brown, Jr.	Colton, CA	714-825-2472
Alfred A. (Al) McCandless	Riverside, CA	714-682-7127
Robert K. Dornan	Garden Grove, CA	714-971-9292
William E. Dannemeyer	Fullerton, CA	714-992-0141
C. Christopher Cox	Newport Beach, CA	714-756-2244
Bill Lowery	San Diego, CA	619-231-0957
Dana Rohrabacher	Los Alamitos, CA	213-761-0517
Ron Packard	Carlsbad, CA	619-438-0443
Jim Bates	San Diego, CA	619-287-8851
Duncan L. Hunter	El Cajon, CA	619-579-3001
GOVERNOR	OFFICE	ADDRESS
George Deukmejian	State Capitol	Sacramento, CA 95814

DIRECTORY OF GOVERNMENT REPRESENTATIVES

	RESIDENCE	ADDRESS
	622 Lake Wilhaggin Drive	Sacramento, CA 95825

COLORADO

SENATORS	DISTRICT OFFICE	TEL. NO.
William L. Armstrong	Denver, CO	303-398-0831
Timothy E. Wirth	Colorado Spring, CO	719-634-5523

REPRESENTATIVES	DISTRICT OFFICE	TEL. NO.
Patricia Schroeder	Denver, CO	303-866-1230
David E. Skaggs	Westminster, CO	303-650-7886
Ben Nighthorse Campbell	Pueblo, CO	303-543-9621
Hank Brown	Greeley, CO	303-352-4112
Joel Hefley	Colorado Springs, CO	303-531-5555
Dan L. Schaefer	Englewood, CO	303-762-8890

GOVERNOR	OFFICE	ADDRESS
Roy Romer	State Capitol	Denver, CO 80203
	RESIDENCE	ADDRESS
	Executive Mansion	Denver, CO 80203

CONNECTICUT

SENATORS	DISTRICT OFFICE	TEL. NO.
Christopher J. Dodd	Wethersfield, CT	203-240-3470
Joe Lieberman	Hartford, CT	203-240-3566

REPRESENTATIVES	DISTRICT OFFICE	TEL. NO.
Barbara B. Kennelly	Hartford, CT	203-278-8888
Sam Gejdenson	Norwich, CT	203-886-0139
Bruce A. Morrison	New Haven, CT	203-773-2325

SURVIVING THE NOT SO GOLDEN YEARS

Christopher Shays	Bridgeport, CT	203-579-5870
John G. Rowland	Waterbury, CT	203-573-1418
Nancy L. Johnson	New Britain, CT	203-223-8412

GOVERNOR	OFFICE	ADDRESS
William A. O'Neill	State Capitol	Hartford, CT 06115
	RESIDENCE	ADDRESS
	Governor's Residence	Hartford, CT 06105

DELAWARE

SENATORS	DISTRICT OFFICE	TEL. NO.
William V. Roth, Jr.	Wilmington, DE	302-573-6291
Joseph R. Biden, Jr.	Wilmington, DE	302-573-6345

REPRESENTATIVES	DISTRICT OFFICE	TEL. NO.
Thomas R. Carper	Wilmington, DE	302-573-6181

GOVERNOR	OFFICE	ADDRESS
Michael N. Castle	Legislative Hall	Dover, DE 19901
	RESIDENCE	ADDRESS
	Governor's Residence	Dover, DE 19901

DISTRICT OF COLUMBIA

DELEGATE	DISTRICT OFFICE	TEL. NO.
Walter E. Fauntroy	Washington, D.C.	202-225-8050

FLORIDA

SENATORS	DISTRICT OFFICE	TEL. NO.
Connie Mack	Tampa, FL	813-289-6777
Bob Graham	Miami, FL	305-536-7293

DIRECTORY OF GOVERNMENT REPRESENTATIVES

REPRESENTATIVES	DISTRICT OFFICE	TEL. NO.
Earl Hutto	Pensacola, FL	904-478-1123
Bill Grant	Tallahassee, FL	904-681-7434
Charles E. Bennett	Jacksonville, FL	904-791-2587
Craig T. James	Daytona, FL	904-239-9823
Bill McCollum	Winter Park, FL	305-645-3100
Cliff Stearns	Ocala, FL	904-351-8011
Sam Gibbons	Tampa, FL	813-228-2101
C.W. Bill Young	St. Petersburg, FL	813-893-3191
Michael Bilirakis	Clearwater, FL	813-441-3721
Andy Ireland	Lakeland, FL	813-687-8018
Bill Nelson	Melbourne, FL	305-676-1776
Tom Lewis	Palm Beach Gardens, FL	305-627-6192
Porter J. Goss	Fort Meyers, FL	813-337-4032
Harry Johnston	W. Palm Beach, FL	407-732-4000
E. Clay Shaw, Jr.	Fort Lauderdale, FL	305-522-1800
Larry J. Smith	Hollywood, FL	305-987-6484
William Lehman	North Miami Beach, FL	305-945-7518
Ileana Ros-Lehtinen	Miami, FL	305-262-1800
Dante B. Fascell	Miami, FL	305-536-5301

GOVERNOR	OFFICE	ADDRESS
Bob Martinez	State Capitol	Tallahassee, FL 32399
	RESIDENCE	ADDRESS
	Governor's Mansion	Tallahassee, FL 32304

GEORGIA

SENATORS	DISTRICT OFFICE	TEL. NO.
Sam Nunn	Atlanta, GA	404-331-4811
Wyche Fowler, Jr.	Atlanta, GA	404-331-0697

REPRESENTATIVES	DISTRICT OFFICE	TEL. NO.
Robert Lindsay Thomas	Savannah, GA	912-944-4360

SURVIVING THE NOT SO GOLDEN YEARS

Charles Hatcher	Albany, GA	912-439-8067
Richard Ray	Columbus, GA	404-324-0292
Ben Jones	Decatur, GA	404-371-9910
John Lewis	Atlanta, GA	404-659-0116
Newt Gingrich	Morrow, GA	404-968-3219
George (Buddy) Darden	Marietta, GA	404-422-4480
J. Roy Rowland	Dublin, GA	912-275-0024
Ed Jenkins	Jasper, GA	404-692-2022
Doug Barnard, Jr.	Augusta, GA	404-724-0739

GOVERNOR	OFFICE	ADDRESS
Joe Frank Harris	State Capitol	Atlanta, GA 30334
	RESIDENCE	ADDRESS
	Governor's Mansion	Atlanta, GA 30305

HAWAII

SENATORS	DISTRICT OFFICE	TEL. NO.
Daniel K. Inouye	Honolulu, HI	808-541-2542
Daniel K. Akaka	Honolulu, HI	808-541-1986

REPRESENTATIVE	DISTRICT OFFICE	TEL. NO.
Patricia Saiki	Honolulu, HI	808-541-2570

GOVERNOR	OFFICE	ADDRESS
John Waihee	State Capitol	Honolulu, HI 96813
	RESIDENCE	ADDRESS
	Washington Place	Honolulu, HI 96813

IDAHO

SENATORS	DISTRICT OFFICE	TEL. NO.
James A. McClure	Boise, ID	208-334-1560

DIRECTORY OF GOVERNMENT REPRESENTATIVES

Steve Symms	Boise, ID	208-334-1776
REPRESENTATIVES	DISTRICT OFFICE	TEL. NO.
Larry E. Craig	Boise, ID	208-342-7985
Richard H. Stallings	Boise, ID	208-344-1953
GOVERNOR	OFFICE	ADDRESS
Cecil D. Andres	State Capitol	Boise, ID 83701
	RESIDENCE	ADDRESS
	1280 Candleridge Dr.	Boise, ID 83712

ILLINOIS

SENATORS	DISTRICT OFFICE	TEL. NO.
Alan L. Dixon	Chicago, IL	312-353-5420
Paul Simon	Chicago, IL	312-353-4952

REPRESENTATIVES	DISTRICT OFFICE	TEL. NO.
Charles A. Hayes	Chicago, IL	312-783-6800
Gus Savage	Chicago, IL	312-660-2000
Marty Russo	Oaklawn, IL	312-353-8093
George E. Sangmeister	Joliet, IL	815-740-2028
William O. Lipinski	Chicago, IL	312-886-0481
Henry J. Hyde	Addison, IL	312-832-5950
Cardiss Collins	Chicago, IL	312-353-5754
Dan Rostenkowski	Chicago, IL	312-431-1111
Sidney R. Yates	Chicago, IL	312-353-4596
John Edward Porter	Deerfield, IL	312-940-0202
Frank Annunzio	Chicago, IL	312-736-0700
Philip M. Crane	Arlington Heights, IL	312-394-0790
Harris W. Fawell	Hinsdale, IL	312-655-2052
J. Dennis Hastert	Batavia, IL	312-406-1114
Edward R. Madigan	Kankakee, IL	815-937-0875
Lynn Martin	Rockford, IL	815-987-4326
Lane Evans	Moline, IL	309-793-5760
Robert M. Michel	Peoria, IL	309-671-7027

SURVIVING THE NOT SO GOLDEN YEARS

Terry L. Bruce	Olney, IL	618-395-8585
Richard J. Durbin	Springfield, IL	217-492-4062
Jerry Costello	Granite City, IL	618-482-9420
Glenn Poshard	West Frankfort, IL	618-937-6402

GOVERNOR	OFFICE	ADDRESS
James R. Thompson	State Capitol	Springfield, IL 62706
	RESIDENCE	ADDRESS
	Executive Mansion	Springfield, IL 62701

INDIANA

SENATORS	DISTRICT OFFICE	TEL. NO.
Richard Lugar	Indianapolis, IN	317-226-5555
Dan Coats	Indianapolis, IN	317-269-5555

REPRESENTATIVES	DISTRICT OFFICE	TEL. NO.
Peter J. Visclosky	Gary, IN	219-884-1177
Philip R. Sharp	Muncie, IN	317-747-5566
John Hiler	South Bend, IN	219-236-8282
Jim Jontz	Kokomo, IN	317-459-4375
Dan Burton	Indianapolis, IN	317-848-0201
John T. Myers	Terre Haute, IN	812-238-1619
Frank McCloskey	Bloomington, IN	812-334-1111
Lee H. Hamilton	Jeffersonville, IN	812-288-3999
Andrew Jacobs, Jr.	Indianapolis, IN	317-269-7331
Jill Long	Fort Wayne, IN	219-424-3041

GOVERNOR	OFFICE	ADDRESS
Evan Bayh	State House	Indianapolis, IN 46204
	RESIDENCE	ADDRESS
	4750 N. Meridian St.	Indianapolis, IN 46208

DIRECTORY OF GOVERNMENT REPRESENTATIVES

IOWA

SENATORS	DISTRICT OFFICE	TEL. NO.
Charles Grassley	Des Moines, IA	515-284-4890
Tom Harkin	Des Moines, IA	515-284-4574

REPRESENTATIVES	DISTRICT OFFICE	TEL. NO.
Jim Leach	Davenport, IA	319-326-1841
Tom Tauke	Dubuque, IA	319-557-7740
David R. Nagle	Waterloo, IA	319-234-3623
Neal Smith	Des Moines, IA	515-284-4634
Jim Lightfoot	Shenandoah, IA	712-246-1984
Fred Grandy	Sioux City, IA	712-252-3733

GOVERNOR	OFFICE	ADDRESS
Terry E. Branstad	State Capitol	Des Moines, IA 50319
	RESIDENCE	ADDRESS
	Executive Mansion	Des Moines, IA 50312

KANSAS

SENATORS	DISTRICT OFFICE	TEL. NO.
Robert Dole	Topeka, KS	913-295-2745
Nancy Kassebaum	Prairie Village, KS	913-648-3103

REPRESENTATIVES	DISTRICT OFFICE	TEL. NO.
Pat Roberts	Dodge City, KS	316-227-2244
Jim Slattery	Topeka, KS	913-295-2811
Jan Meyers	Kansas City, KS	913-621-0832
Dan Glickman	Wichita, KS	913-262-8396
Bob Whittaker	Augusta, KS	316-775-1127

GOVERNOR	OFFICE	ADDRESS
Mike Hayden	State Capitol	Topeka, KS 66612

	RESIDENCE	ADDRESS
	Cedar Crest	Topeka, KS 66606

KENTUCKY

SENATORS	DISTRICT OFFICE	TEL. NO.
Wendall H. Ford	Louisville, KY	502-582-6251
Mitch McConnell	Louisville, KY	502-582-6304

REPRESENTATIVES	DISTRICT OFFICE	TEL. NO.
Carroll Hubbard, Jr.	Paducah, KY	502-442-9806
William H. Natcher	Bowling Green, KY	502-842-7376
Romano L. Mazzoli	Louisville, KY	502-582-5129
Jim Bunning	Fort Wright, KY	606-341-2602
Harold Rogers	Somerset, KY	606-679-8346
Larry J. Hopkins	Lexington, KY	606-233-2848
Carl C. Perkins	Morehead, KY	606-784-1000

GOVERNOR	OFFICE	ADDRESS
Wallace Wilkinson	State Capitol	Frankfort, KY 40601
	RESIDENCE	ADDRESS
	Executive Mansion	Frankfort, KY 40601

LOUISIANA

SENATORS	DISTRICT OFFICE	TEL. NO.
J. Bennett Johnston	Shreveport, LA	318-226-5085
John B. Breaux	New Orleans, LA	504-589-2531

REPRESENTATIVES	DISTRICT OFFICE	TEL. NO.
Bob Livingston	Metairie, LA	504-589-2753
Lindy Boggs	New Orleans, LA	504-589-2274
W.J. (Billy) Tauzin	Houma, LA	504-876-3033
Jim McCrery	Shreveport, LA	318-226-5080
Jerry Huckaby	Monroe, LA	318-387-2244

DIRECTORY OF GOVERNMENT REPRESENTATIVES

Richard Baker	Baton Rouge, LA	504-929-7711
Jimmy Hayes	Lafayette, LA	318-233-4773
Clyde Holloway	Alexandria, LA	318-473-7430

GOVERNOR	OFFICE	ADDRESS
Buddy Roemer	P.O. Box 94004	Baton Rouge, LA 70804
	RESIDENCE	ADDRESS
	Governor's Mansion	Baton Rouge, LA 70802

MAINE

SENATORS	DISTRICT OFFICE	TEL. NO.
William S. Cohen	Bangor, ME	207-947-0417
George J. Mitchell	Portland, ME	207-780-3561

REPRESENTATIVES	DISTRICT OFFICE	TEL. NO.
Joseph E. Brennan	Portland, ME	207-772-8240
Olympia J. Snowe	Auburn, ME	207-786-2451

GOVERNOR	OFFICE	ADDRESS
John R. McKearnan, Jr.	State House	Augusta, ME 04333
	RESIDENCE	ADDRESS
	Blaine House	Augusta, ME 04330

MARYLAND

SENATORS	DISTRICT OFFICE	TEL. NO.
Paul S. Sarbanes	Baltimore, MD	301-962-4436
Barbara Mikulski	Baltimore, MD	301-962-4510

REPRESENTATIVES	DISTRICT OFFICE	TEL. NO.
Roy Dyson	Salisbury, MD	301-742-9070
Helen Delich Bentley	Towson, MD	301-337-7222

SURVIVING THE NOT SO GOLDEN YEARS

Benjamin L. Cardin	Baltimore, MD	301-433-8886
Thomas McMillen	Glen Burnie, MD	301-768-8050
Steny H. Hoyer	Landover, MD	301-436-5510
Beverly B. Byron	Frederick, MD	301-662-8622
Kweisi Mfume	Baltimore, MD	301-367-1900
Constance A. Morella	Wheaton, MD	301-946-6801

GOVERNOR	OFFICE	ADDRESS
William Donald Schaefer	State House	Annapolis, MD 21401
	RESIDENCE	ADDRESS
	Government House	Annapolis, MD 21401

MASSACHUSETTS

SENATORS	DISTRICT OFFICE	TEL. NO.
Edward M. Kennedy	Hyannis Port, MA	617-565-3170
John F. Kerry	Boston, MA	617-565-8519

REPRESENTATIVES	DISTRICT OFFICE	TEL. NO.
Silvio O. Conte	Pittsfield, MA	413-442-0946
Richard E. Neal	Springfield, MA	413-785-0325
Joseph D. Early	Worcester, MA	617-752-6718
Barney Frank	Newton, MA	617-332-3920
Chester G. Atkins	Lowell, MA	508-459-0101
Nicholas Mavroules	Salem, MA	617-745-5800
Edward J. Markey	Boston, MA	617-565-2900
Joseph P. Kennedy II	Boston, MA	617-565-8686
Joe Moakley	Boston, MA	617-565-2920
Gerry E. Studds	New Bedford, MA	508-999-1251
Brian J. Donnelly	Boston, MA	617-565-2910

GOVERNOR	OFFICE	ADDRESS
Michael S. Dukakis	State House	Boston, MA 02133

DIRECTORY OF GOVERNMENT REPRESENTATIVES

	RESIDENCE	ADDRESS
	85 Perry Street	Brookline, MA 02146

MICHIGAN

SENATORS	DISTRICT OFFICE	TEL. NO.
Donald Riegle	Lansing, MI	517-377-1713
Carl Levin	Detroit, MI	313-226-6020

REPRESENTATIVES	DISTRICT OFFICE	TEL. NO.
John Conyers	Detroit, MI	313-961-5670
Carl D. Pursell	Ann Arbor, MI	313-761-7727
Howard Wolpe	Lansing, MI	517-377-1644
Fred Upton	St. Joseph, MI	616-982-1986
Paul B. Henry	Grand Rapids, MI	616-451-8383
Bob Carr	East Lansing, MI	517-351-7203
Dale E. Kildee	Flint, MI	313-239-1437
Bob Traxler	Saginaw, MI	517-754-4226
Guy Vander Jagt	Muskegon, MI	616-733-3131
Bill Schuette	Midland, MI	517-631-2552
Robert W. Davis	Marquette, MI	906-228-3700
David E. Bonior	Mount Clemens, MI	313-469-3232
George W. Crockett	Detroit, MI	313-874-4900
Dennis M. Hertel	Detroit, MI	313-526-5900
William D. Ford	Wayne, MI	313-722-1411
John D. Dingell	Dearborn, MI	313-846-1276
Sander M. Levin	Southfield, MI	313-559-4444
William S. Broomfield	Birmingham, MI	313-642-3800

GOVERNOR	OFFICE	ADDRESS
James Blanchard	State Capitol	Lansing, MI 48913
	RESIDENCE	ADDRESS
	Governor's Residence	Lansing, MI 48910

SURVIVING THE NOT SO GOLDEN YEARS

MINNESOTA

SENATORS	DISTRICT OFFICE	TEL. NO.
Dave Durenberger	Minneapolis, MN	612-349-5111
Rudy Boschwitz	St. Paul, MN	612-221-0904

REPRESENTATIVES	DISTRICT OFFICE	TEL. NO.
Timothy J. Penny	Rochester, MN	507-281-6053
Vin Weber	New Ulm, MN	507-354-6400
Bill Frenzel	Bloomington, MN	612-881-6400
Bruce F. Vento	St. Paul, MN	612-224-4503
Martin Olav Sabo	Minneapolis, MN	612-348-1649
Gerry Sikorski	Fridley, MN	612-780-5801
Arlen Strangeland	Moorehead, MN	218-233-8631
James L. Oberstar	Duluth, MN	218-727-7474

GOVERNOR	OFFICE	ADDRESS
Rudy Perpich	State Capitol	St. Paul, MN 55155
	RESIDENCE	ADDRESS
	Governor's Residence	St. Paul, MN 55105

MISSISSIPPI

SENATORS	DISTRICT OFFICE	TEL. NO.
Trent Lott	Jackson, MS	601-965-4644
Thad Cochran	Jackson, MS	601-965-4459

REPRESENTATIVES	DISTRICT OFFICE	TEL. NO.
Jamie L. Whitten	Charleston, MS	601-647-2413
Mike Espy	Yazoo City, MS	601-746-1400
G.V. "Sonny" Montgomery	Meridian, MS	601-693-6681
Mike Parker	Jackson, MS	601-965-4085
Gene Taylor	Gulfport, MS	601-864-7670

DIRECTORY OF GOVERNMENT REPRESENTATIVES

GOVERNOR	OFFICE	ADDRESS
Ray Mabus	P.O. Box 139	Jackson, MS 39205
	RESIDENCE	ADDRESS
	Governor's Mansion	Jackson, MS 39201

MISSOURI

SENATORS	DISTRICT OFFICE	TEL. NO.
John C. Danforth	St. Louis, MO	314-425-6381
Christopher S. "Kit" Bond	Jefferson, MO	314-634-2488

REPRESENTATIVES	DISTRICT OFFICE	TEL. NO.
William (Bill) Clay	St. Louis, MO	314-725-5770
Jack Buechner	Ballwin, MO	314-965-1101
Richard A. Gephardt	St. Louis, MO	314-639-9959
Ike Skelton	Blue Springs, MO	816-228-4242
Alan Wheat	Kansas City, MO	816-842-4545
E. Thomas Coleman	Kansas City, MO	816-454-7117
Melton "Mel" Hancock	Springfield, MO	417-862-4317
Bill Emerson	Cape Girandeau, MO	314-335-0101
Harold L. Volkmer	Hannibal, MO	314-221-1200

GOVERNOR	OFFICE	ADDRESS
John Ashcroft	P.O. Box 720	Jefferson City, MO 65102
	RESIDENCE	ADDRESS
	Governor's Residence	Jefferson City, MO 65101

MONTANA

SENATORS	DISTRICT OFFICE	TEL. NO.
Conrad Burns	Billings, MT	406-252-0550

SURVIVING THE NOT SO GOLDEN YEARS

Max Baucus	Great Falls, MT	406-761-1574
REPRESENTATIVES	DISTRICT OFFICE	TEL. NO.
Pat Williams	Helena, MT	406-443-7878
Ron Marlenee	Billings, MT	406-657-6753
GOVERNOR	OFFICE	ADDRESS
Stan Stephens	State Capitol	Helena, MT 59620
	RESIDENCE	ADDRESS
	Executive Mansion	Helena, MT 59601

NEBRASKA

SENATORS	DISTRICT OFFICE	TEL. NO.
J. James Exon	Lincoln, NE	402-437-5591
Bob Kerrey	Omaha, NE	402-391-3411
REPRESENTATIVES	DISTRICT OFFICE	TEL. NO.
Doug Bereuter	Lincoln, NE	402-437-5400
Pete Hoagland	Omaha, NE	402-221-4216
Virginia Smith	Scotts Bluff, NE	308-632-3333
GOVERNOR	OFFICE	ADDRESS
Kay A. Orr	State Capitol	Lincoln, NE 68509
	RESIDENCE	ADDRESS
	Governor's Mansion	Lincoln, NE 68508

NEVADA

SENATORS	DISTRICT OFFICE	TEL. NO.
Richard H. Bryan	Las Vegas, NV	702-388-6666
Harry Reid	Las Vegas, NV	702-388-6545

DIRECTORY OF GOVERNMENT REPRESENTATIVES

REPRESENTATIVES	DISTRICT OFFICE	TEL. NO.
James H. Bilbray	Las Vegas, NV	702-477-7000
Barbara F. Vucanovich	Reno, NV	702-784-5003
GOVERNOR	OFFICE	ADDRESS
Robert J. Miller	State Capitol	Carson City, NV 89710
	RESIDENCE	ADDRESS
	Governor's Mansion	Carson City, NV 89710

NEW HAMPSHIRE

SENATORS	DISTRICT OFFICE	TEL. NO.
Gordon Humphrey	Concord, NH	603-228-0453
Warren B. Rudman	Concord, NH	603-225-7115
REPRESENTATIVES	DISTRICT OFFICE	TEL. NO.
Robert C. Smith	Manchester, NH	603-644-3387
Chuck Douglas	Concord, NH	603-225-9693
GOVERNOR	OFFICE	ADDRESS
Judd Gregg	State House	Concord, NH 03301
	RESIDENCE	ADDRESS
	Drawer I	Greenfield, NH 03047

NEW JERSEY

SENATORS	DISTRICT OFFICE	TEL. NO.
Bill Bradley	Union, NJ	201-688-0960
Frank R. Lautenberg	Newark, NJ	201-645-3030
REPRESENTATIVES	DISTRICT OFFICE	TEL. NO.
William J. Hughes	Northfield, NJ	609-645-7957
Frank Pallone	Long Branch, NJ	201-570-1140

SURVIVING THE NOT SO GOLDEN YEARS

Christopher H. Smith	Trenton, NJ	609-890-2800
Marge Roukema	Ridgewood, NJ	201-447-3900
Bernard J. Dwyer	Perth Amboy, NJ	201-826-4610
Matthew J. Rinaldo	Union, NJ	201-687-4235
Robert A. Roe	Wayne, NJ	201-696-2077
Robert G. Torricelli	Hackensack, NJ	201-646-1111
Donald M. Payne	Newark, NJ	201-645-3213
Dean A. Gallo	Parsipanny, NJ	201-984-0711
Jim Courter	Morristown, NJ	201-538-7267
James H. Saxton	Mt. Holly, NJ	609-261-5800
Frank J. Guarini	Jersey City, NJ	201-659-7700

GOVERNOR	OFFICE	ADDRESS
James J. Florio	State House	Trenton, NJ 08625
	RESIDENCE	ADDRESS
	Drumthwacket	Princeton, NJ 08540

NEW MEXICO

SENATORS	DISTRICT OFFICE	TEL. NO.
Pete V. Domenici	Albuquerque, NM	505-766-3481
Jeff Bingaman	Albuquerque, NM	505-766-3636

REPRESENTATIVES	DISTRICT OFFICE	TEL. NO.
Steven Schiff	Albuquerque, NM	505-766-2538
Joe Skeen	Rosell, NM	505-622-0055
Bill Richardson	Santa Fe, NM	505-988-6177

GOVERNOR	OFFICE	ADDRESS
Garry E. Carruthers	State Capitol	Sante Fe, NM 87503
	RESIDENCE	ADDRESS
	Governor's Residence	Santa Fe, NM 87501

DIRECTORY OF GOVERNMENT REPRESENTATIVES

NEW YORK

SENATORS	DISTRICT OFFICE	TEL. NO.
Daniel Patrick Moynihan	New York City, NY	212-661-5150
Alfonse D'Amato	New York City, NY	212-947-7390

REPRESENTATIVES	DISTRICT OFFICE	TEL. NO.
George J. Hochbrueckner	Centereach, NY	516-689-6767
Thomas J. Downey	West Islip, NY	516-661-8777
Robert J. Mrazek	Huntington, NY	516-673-6500
Norman F. Lent	Baldwin, NY	516-223-1616
Floyd H. Flake	Jamaica, NY	718-657-2968
Gary L. Ackerman	Forest Hills, NY	718-263-1525
James H. Scheuer	Flushing, NY	718-445-8770
Thomas J. Manton	Sunnyside, NY	718-706-1400
Charles E. Schumer	Brooklyn, NY	718-965-5400
Edolphus Towns	Brooklyn, NY	718-622-5700
Major R. Owens	Brooklyn, NY	718-773-3100
Stephen R. Solarz	Brooklyn, NY	718-372-8600
Bill Green	Manhattan, NY	212-826-4466
Charles B. Rangel	New York City, NY	212-663-3900
Ted Weiss	New York City, NY	212-620-3970
Eliot L. Engel	Bronx, NY	212-320-2314
		212-823-7200
Nita M. Lowey	White Plains, NY	914-428-1707
Hamilton Fish, Jr.	Poughkeepsie, NY	914-452-4220
Benjamin A. Gilman	Middletown, NY	914-343-6666
Michael R. McNulty	Schenectady, NY	518-374-4547
Gerald B.H. Solomon	Saratoga Springs, NY	518-587-9800
Sherwood Boehlert	Utica, NY	315-793-8146
David O'B. Martin	Canton, NY	315-379-9611
James T. Walsh	Syracuse, NY	315-423-5657
Matthew F. McHugh	Ithaca, NY	607-273-1388
Frank Horton	Rochester, NY	716-454-7490
Louise M. Slaughter	Rochester, NY	716-232-4850
Bill Paxon	Amherst, NY	716-648-2324

SURVIVING THE NOT SO GOLDEN YEARS

John J. LaFalce	Buffalo, NY	716-846-4056
Henry J. Nowak	Buffalo, NY	716-853-4131
Amory Houghton, Jr.	Corning, NY	607-937-3333
Raymond McGrath	Valley Stream, NY	516-872-9550

GOVERNOR	OFFICE	ADDRESS
Mario M. Cuomo	State Capitol	Albany, NY 12224
	RESIDENCE	ADDRESS
	Executive Mansion	Albany, NY 12224

NORTH CAROLINA

SENATORS	DISTRICT OFFICE	TEL. NO.
Jesse Helms	Raleigh, NC	919-856-4630
Terry Sanford	Raleigh, NC	919-856-4401

REPRESENTATIVES	DISTRICT OFFICE	TEL. NO.
Walter B. Jones	Farmville, NC	919-753-3082
Tim Valentine	Durham, NC	919-541-5201
H. Martin Lancaster	Goldsboro, NC	919-736-1844
David E. Price	Raleigh, NC	919-856-4611
Stephen L. Neal	Winston-Salem, NC	919-631-5125
Howard Coble	Greensboro, NC	919-335-5005
Charlie Rose	Fayetteville, NC	919-323-0260
W.G. (Bill) Hefner	Concord, NC	704-933-1615
J. Alex McMillan	Charlotte, NC	704-372-1976
Cass Ballenger	Hickory, NC	704-327-6100
James McClure Clarke	Ashville, NC	704-254-1747

GOVERNOR	OFFICE	ADDRESS
James G. Martin	State Capitol	Raleigh, NC 27611
	RESIDENCE	ADDRESS
	Executive Mansion	Raleigh, NC 27601

DIRECTORY OF GOVERNMENT REPRESENTATIVES

NORTH DAKOTA

SENATORS	DISTRICT OFFICE	TEL. NO.
Quentin N. Burdick	Fargo, ND	701-237-4000
Kent Conrad	Bismarck, ND	701-258-4648

REPRESENTATIVES	DISTRICT OFFICE	TEL. NO.
Byron L. Dorgan	Bismarck, ND	701-250-4618

GOVERNOR	OFFICE	ADDRESS
George A. Sinner	State Capitol	Bismarck, ND 58505
	RESIDENCE	ADDRESS
	Governor's Residence	Bismarck, ND 58505

OHIO

SENATORS	DISTRICT OFFICE	TEL. NO.
John Glenn	Columbus, OH	614-469-6697
Howard M. Metzenbaum	Cleveland, OH	216-522-7272

REPRESENTATIVES	DISTRICT OFFICE	TEL. NO.
Thomas A. Luken	Cincinnati, OH	513-684-2723
Willis Gradison, Jr.	Cincinnati, OH	513-684-2456
Tony P. Hall	Dayton, OH	513-225-2843
Michael G. Oxley	Lima, OH	419-999-6455
Paul E. Gillmor	Bowling Green, OH	419-354-1988
Bob McEwen	Hillsboro, OH	513-393-4223
Michael DeWine	Springfield, OH	513-325-0474
Donald "Buz" Lukens	Hamilton, OH	513-895-5656
Marcy Kaptur	Toledo, OH	419-259-7500
Clarence E. Miller	Lancaster, OH	614-654-5149
Dennis E. Eckart	Mentor, OH	216-522-2056
John R. Kasich	Columbus, OH	614-469-7318
Donald J. Pease	Lorain, OH	216-282-5003
Thomas Sawyer	Akron, OH	216-375-5710

SURVIVING THE NOT SO GOLDEN YEARS

Chalmers P. Wylie	Columbus, OH	614-469-5614
Ralph Regula	Canton, OH	216-489-4414
James Traficant, Jr.	Youngstown, OH	216-788-2414
Douglas Applegate	Steubenville, OH	614-283-3716
Edward F. Feighan	Cleveland, OH	216-522-4382
Mary Rose Oakar	Cleveland, OH	216-522-4927
Louis Stokes	Cleveland, OH	216-522-4900

GOVERNOR	OFFICE	ADDRESS
Richard F. Celeste	State House	Columbus, OH 43215
	RESIDENCE	ADDRESS
	358 N. Parkview	Bexley, OH 43209

OKLAHOMA

SENATORS	DISTRICT OFFICE	TEL. NO.
David L. Boren	Oklahoma City, OK	405-231-4381
Don Nickles	Oklahoma City, OK	405-231-4941

REPRESENTATIVES	DISTRICT OFFICE	TEL. NO.
James M. Inhofe	Tulsa, OK	918-581-7111
Mike Synar	Muskogee, OK	918-687-2533
Wes Watkins	Ada, OK	405-436-1980
Dave McCurdy	Norman, OK	405-329-6500
Mickey Edwards	Oklahoma City, OK	405-231-4541
Glenn English	Oklahoma City, OK	405-231-5511

GOVERNOR	OFFICE	ADDRESS
Henry Bellmon	State Capitol	Oklahoma City, OK 73105
	RESIDENCE	ADDRESS
	State Capitol	Oklahoma City, OK 73105

OREGON

SENATORS	DISTRICT OFFICE	TEL. NO.
Mark O. Hatfield	Portland, OR	503-221-3386
Bob Packwood	Portland, OR	503-221-3370

REPRESENTATIVES	DISTRICT OFFICE	TEL. NO.
Les AuCoin	Portland, OR	503-326-2901
Robert F. Smith	Medford, OR	503-776-4646
Ron Wyden	Portland, OR	503-231-2300
Pete A. DeFazio	Eugene, OR	503-687-6732
Denny Smith	Salem, OR	503-399-5756

GOVERNOR	OFFICE	ADDRESS
Neil Goldschmidt	State Capitol	Salem, OR 97310
	RESIDENCE	ADDRESS
	533 Lincoln St. S.	Salem, OR 97302-5128

PENNSYLVANIA

SENATORS	DISTRICT OFFICE	TEL. NO.
John Heinz	Pittsburgh, PA	412-562-0533
Arlen Specter	Philadelphia, PA	215-597-7200

REPRESENTATIVES	DISTRICT OFFICE	TEL. NO.
Thomas M. Foglietta	Philadelphia, PA	215-925-6840
William H. Gray III	Philadelphia, PA	215-951-5388
Robert A. Borski	Philadelphia, PA	215-335-3355
Joe Kolter	Beaver Falls, PA	412-846-3600
Richard T. Schulze	Paoli, PA	215-648-0555
Gus Yatron	Reading, PA	215-929-9233
Curt Weldon	Upper Darby, PA	215-259-0700
Peter H. Kostmayer	Doylestown, PA	215-345-8543
Bud Shuster	Altoona, PA	814-946-1653
Joseph M. McDade	Scranton, PA	717-346-3834
Paul E. Kanjorski	Wilkes-Barre, PA	717-825-2200
John P. Murtha	Johnstown, PA	814-535-2642

SURVIVING THE NOT SO GOLDEN YEARS

Lawrence Coughlin	Morristown, PA	215-277-4040
William J. Coyne	Pittsburgh, PA	412-644-2870
Don Ritter	Bethlehem, PA	215-866-0916
Robert S. Walker	Lancaster, PA	717-393-0666
George W. Gekas	Harrisburg, PA	717-232-5123
Doug Walgren	Pittsburgh, PA	412-391-4016
Bill Goodling	York, PA	717-843-8887
Joseph M. Gaydos	McKeesport, PA	412-644-2860
Tom Ridge	Erie, PA	814-456-2038
Austin J. Murphy	Charleroi, PA	412-489-4217
William Clinger, Jr.	Warren, PA	814-726-3910

GOVERNOR	OFFICE	ADDRESS
Robert P. Casey	225 Main Capitol Bldg.	Harrisburg, PA 17120
	RESIDENCE	ADDRESS
	2035 N. Front St.	Harrisburg, PA 17102

RHODE ISLAND

SENATORS	DISTRICT OFFICE	TEL. NO.
Claiborne Pell	Providence, RI	401-528-5456
John H. Chafee	Providence, RI	401-528-5294

REPRESENTATIVES	DISTRICT OFFICE	TEL. NO.
Donald K. Machtley	Pawtucket, RI	401-725-9400
Claudine Schneider	Cranston, RI	401-528-5020

GOVERNOR	OFFICE	ADDRESS
Edward D. DiPrete	State House	Providence, RI 02903
	RESIDENCE	ADDRESS
	555 Wilbur Avenue	Cranston, RI 02920

DIRECTORY OF GOVERNMENT REPRESENTATIVES

SOUTH CAROLINA

SENATORS	DISTRICT OFFICE	TEL. NO.
Strom Thurmond	Columbia, SC	803-765-5496
Ernest F. Hollings	Columbia, SC	803-765-5731

REPRESENTATIVES	DISTRICT OFFICE	TEL. NO.
Arthur Ravenel, Jr.	Charleston, SC	803-724-4175
Floyd Spence	Columbia, SC	803-254-5120
Butler Derrick	Anderson, SC	803-224-7401
Elizabeth J. Patterson	Greenville, SC	803-232-1141
John M. Spratt, Jr.	Rock Hill, SC	803-327-1114
Robin Tallon	Florence, SC	803-669-9084

GOVERNOR	OFFICE	ADDRESS
Carroll Campbell, Jr.	P.O. Box 12428	Columbia, SC 29211
	RESIDENCE	ADDRESS
	Governor's Mansion	Columbia, SC 29201

SOUTH DAKOTA

SENATORS	DISTRICT OFFICE	TEL. NO.
Larry Pressler	Sioux Falls, SD	605-336-2980
Thomas A. Daschle	Sioux Falls, SD	605-334-9596

REPRESENTATIVES	DISTRICT OFFICE	TEL. NO.
Tim Johnson	Sioux Falls, SD	605-332-8896

GOVERNOR	OFFICE	ADDRESS
George S. Mickelson	State Capitol	Pierre, SD 57501
	RESIDENCE	ADDRESS
	Governor's Mansion	Pierre, SD 57501

TENNESSEE

SENATORS	DISTRICT OFFICE	TEL. NO.
Jim Sasser	Nashville, TN	615-736-7353
Albert Gore	Nashville, TN	615-736-5129

REPRESENTATIVES	DISTRICT OFFICE	TEL. NO.
James H. Quillen	Kingsport, TN	615-247-8161
John J. Duncan	Knoxville, TN	615-673-4282
Marilyn Lloyd	Chattanooga, TN	615-267-9108
Jim Cooper	Shelbyville, TN	615-684-1114
Bob Clement	Nashville, TN	615-736-5295
Bart Gordon	Murfreesboro, TN	615-896-1986
Don Sundquist	Memphis, TN	901-382-5811
John Tanner	Jackson, TN	901-423-4848
Harold E. Ford	Memphis, TN	901-521-4131

GOVERNOR	OFFICE	ADDRESS
Ned Ray McWherter	State Capitol	Nashville, TN 37219
	RESIDENCE	ADDRESS
	Executive Residence	Nashville, TN 37204

TEXAS

SENATORS	DISTRICT OFFICE	TEL. NO.
Lloyd Bentsen	Austin, TX	512-482-5834
Phil Gramm	Dallas, TX	214-767-3000

REPRESENTATIVES	DISTRICT OFFICE	TEL. NO.
Jim Chapman	Sulphur Springs, TX	214-885-8682
Charles Wilson	Lufkin, TX	409-637-1770
Steve Bartlett	Dallas, TX	214-767-4848
Ralph M. Hall	Rockwall, TX	214-771-9118
John Bryant	Dallas, TX	214-767-6554
Joe L. Barton	Ft. Worth, TX	817-737-7737
Bill Archer	Houston, TX	713-467-7493
Jack Fields	Houston, TX	713-451-6334

DIRECTORY OF GOVERNMENT REPRESENTATIVES

Jack Brooks	Beaumont, TX	409-839-2508
J.J. Pickle	Austin, TX	512-482-5921
Marvin Leath	Waco, TX	817-752-9600
Pete Geren	Fort Worth, TX	817-338-0909
Bill Sarpalius	Amarillo, TX	806-371-8841
Greg Laughlin	Victoria, TX	512-576-6001
E. (Kika) de la Garza	McAllen, TX	512-682-5545
Ronald D. Coleman	El Paso, TX	915-534-6200
Charles W. Stenholm	Stamford, TX	915-773-3623
Craig Washington	Houston, TX	713-739-7339
Larry Combest	Lubbock, TX	806-763-1611
Henry B. Gonzalez	San Antonio, TX	512-229-6195
Lamar Smith	San Antonio, TX	512-229-5880
Thomas D. DeLay	Houston, TX	713-270-4000
Albert G. Bustamante	San Antonio, TX	512-229-6191
Martin Frost	Dallas, TX	214-767-2816
Michael A. Andrews	Houston, TX	713-229-2244
Dick K. Armey	Lewisville, TX	214-221-4527
Solomon P. Ortiz	Corpus Christi, TX	512-883-5868

GOVERNOR	OFFICE	ADDRESS
William Clements, Jr.	P.O. Box 12428	Austin, TX 78711
	RESIDENCE	ADDRESS
	Governor's Mansion	Austin, TX 78701

UTAH

SENATORS	DISTRICT OFFICE	TEL. NO.
Jake Garn	Salt Lake City, UT	801-524-5933
Orrin Hatch	Salt Lake City, UT	801-524-4380

REPRESENTATIVES	DISTRICT OFFICE	TEL. NO.
James Hansen	Ogden, UT	801-625-5670

SURVIVING THE NOT SO GOLDEN YEARS

Wayne Owens	Salt Lake City, UT	801-524-4394
Howard C. Nielson	Provo, UT	801-377-1776

GOVERNOR	OFFICE	ADDRESS
Norman H. Bangerter	State Capitol	Salt Lake City, UT 84114
	RESIDENCE	ADDRESS
	Executive Residence	Salt Lake City, UT 84102

VERMONT

SENATORS	DISTRICT OFFICE	TEL. NO.
James M. Jeffords	Minooski, VT	802-951-6732
Patrick Leahy	Burlington, VT	802-863-2525

REPRESENTATIVE	DISTRICT OFFICE	TEL. NO.
Peter Smith	Rutland, VT	802-773-5790

GOVERNOR	OFFICE	ADDRESS
Madeleine M. Kunin	Pavilion Office Bldg.	Montpelier, VT 05602
	RESIDENCE	ADDRESS
	122 Dunder Road	Burlington, VT 05401

VIRGINIA

SENATORS	DISTRICT OFFICE	TEL. NO.
John Warner	Richmond, VA	804-771-2579
Charles S. Robb	Richmond, VA	804-771-2221

REPRESENTATIVES	DISTRICT OFFICE	TEL. NO.
Herbert H. Bateman	Newport News, VA	804-873-1132
Owen B. Pickett	Norfolk, VA	804-624-9124
Thomas J. Bliley, Jr.	Richmond, VA	804-771-2809
Norman Sisisky	Portsmouth, VA	804-393-2068
Lewis F. Payne, Jr.	Danville, VA	804-792-1280

DIRECTORY OF GOVERNMENT REPRESENTATIVES

Jim Olin	Roanoke, VA	703-982-4672
D. French Slaughter	Culpeper, VA	703-825-3495
Stan Parris	Springfield, VA	703-644-0004
Frederick C. Boucher	Abingdon, VA	703-628-1145
Frank R. Wolf	McLean, VA	703-734-1500

GOVERNOR	OFFICE	ADDRESS
Gerald Baliles	State Capitol	Richmond, VA 23219
	RESIDENCE	ADDRESS
	Executive Mansion	Richmond, VA 23219

WASHINGTON

SENATORS	DISTRICT OFFICE	TEL. NO.
Slade Gorton	Seattle, WA	206-442-0350
Brock Adams	Seattle, WA	206-442-5545

REPRESENTATIVES	DISTRICT OFFICE	TEL. NO.
John Miller	Seattle, WA	206-442-4220
Al Swift	Everett, WA	206-252-3188
Jolene Unsoeld	Olympia, WA	206-753-9528
Sid Morrison	Yakima, WA	509-575-5891
Thomas S. Foley	Spokane, WA	509-456-4680
Norman D. Dicks	Bremerton, WA	206-479-4011
Jim McDermott	Seattle, WA	206-442-7170
Rod Chandler	Bellevue, WA	206-442-0116

GOVERNOR	OFFICE	ADDRESS
Booth Gardner	Legislative Bldg.	Olympia, WA 98504
	RESIDENCE	ADDRESS
	Executive Mansion	Olympia, WA 98501

SURVIVING THE NOT SO GOLDEN YEARS

WEST VIRGINIA

SENATORS	DISTRICT OFFICE	TEL. NO.
Robert C. Byrd	Charleston, WV	304-342-5855
John D. (Jay) Rockefeller IV	Charleston, WV	304-347-5372

REPRESENTATIVES	DISTRICT OFFICE	TEL. NO.
Alan B. Mollohan	Fairmont, WV	304-363-3356
Harley Staggers, Jr.	Morgantown, WV	304-291-6001
Robert E. Wise, Jr.	Charleston, WV	304-342-7170
Nick Joe Rahall II	Beckley, WV	304-252-5000

GOVERNOR	OFFICE	ADDRESS
Guston Caperton	State Capitol	Charleston, WV 25305
	RESIDENCE	ADDRESS
	Governor's Mansion	Charleston, WV 25305

WISCONSIN

SENATORS	DISTRICT OFFICE	TEL. NO.
Herbert H. Kohl	Madison, WI	608-264-5472
Robert W. Kasten, Jr.	Milwaukee, WI	414-291-4160

REPRESENTATIVES	DISTRICT OFFICE	TEL. NO.
Les Aspin	Racine, WI	414-632-4446
Robert W. Kastenmeir	Madison, WI	608-264-5206
Steve Gunderson	Black River Falls, WI	715-284-7431
Gerald D. Kleczka	Milwaukee, WI	414-291-1140
Jim Moody	Milwaukee, WI	414-291-1331
Thomas E. Petri	Fond du Lac, WI	414-922-1180
David R. Obey	Wausau, WI	715-842-5606
Toby Roth	Appleton, WI	414-739-4167

DIRECTORY OF GOVERNMENT REPRESENTATIVES

F. James
   Sensenbrenner, Jr. Brookfield, WI   414-784-1111

GOVERNOR	OFFICE	ADDRESS
Tommy G. Thompson	State Capitol	Madison, WI 53702
	RESIDENCE	ADDRESS
	Executive Residence	Madison, WI 53704

WYOMING

SENATORS	DISTRICT OFFICE	TEL. NO.
Malcom Wallop	Cheyenne, WY	307-634-0626
Alan K. Simpson	Cody, WY	307-527-7121

REPRESENTATIVE	DISTRICT OFFICE	TEL. NO.
Craig Thomas	Casper, WY	307-261-5413

GOVERNOR	OFFICE	ADDRESS
Michael Sullivan	State Capitol	Cheyenne, WY 82002
	RESIDENCE	ADDRESS
	Governor's Residence	Cheyenne, WY 82009

AFTERWORD

Subsequent to the completion of this book, my mother passed away. Again it felt as if we had learned a valuable lesson, a lesson that was tragically learned at my mother's and the family's expense. Mother lived and died without the benefit of a designated durable Power of Attorney and a Living Will. A few short years ago there was little or no awareness of either of these and it never crossed our minds to have them drawn up on her behalf.

Also, Mother was a resident of Florida, where the efficacy of these two documents is still questionable. Nevertheless, when the time came and considering the circumstances of Mother's death, we deeply regretted not having the legal documents expressing her intent, as having them might have made the last hours of Mother's life a little less painful for everyone.

GLOSSARY

Applicant—the individual who is applying for Medicaid.

Calendar month—in the context of Medicaid regulations refers to the first full month after a person has entered a nursing home facility. For example, a person who enters a nursing home on January 23 is considered an individual separate and apart from the spouse, for financial purposes, starting February 1.

Community spouse—this refers to the spouse who will be remaining in the home as opposed to the institutionalized spouse.

Countable resources—these are assets which belong to the Medicaid applicant and which are considered by Medicaid when determining financial eligibility.

Deeming—is the process of transferring money from one spouse to another.

Durational residency—in the context of this book means having to reside in a state for a specified period of time, in order to qualify as a resident.

Exemptions—personal belongings and effects that are not considered by Medicaid in determining eligibility of the applicant.

Fixed assets—real estate, property, automobiles, or assets that cannot be readily liquidated.

Homestead—in the context of Medicaid, is the primary residence, house, apartment, condominium where the applicant lives.

Household goods—items in the home, of any significant financial value.

Institutionalized spouse—the spouse who is currently residing in a nursing home facility.

Intermediate-care facility—a facility where the level of care is supervised personal care and health related services under a physician's direction. Care can usually be provided by trained aides and orderlies under the supervision of a licensed practical nurse. Facilities providing this level of care are required to have licensed nurses 24 hours a day, seven days a week. There are also intermediate-care facilities, where the medical needs are not as intense, and they are required to have licensed nurses only 12 hours a day, seven days a week.

Irrevocable—something that cannot be retracted or undone, e.g., a contract or a deed.

Liquid assets—generally applies to such resources as cash on hand, savings and checking accounts, stocks, bonds, mutual funds, and CDs (certificates of deposit).

Medically needy—elderly individuals (65 or over) who, because of limited income and resources, need help in paying their medical bills and, because they do not receive financial assistance from the state or SSI, fall into the category of medically needy in some states.

Personal effects—items or personal possessions which are of significant financial value, e.g., jewelry, etc.

Probate—the process of proving that a will is real and valid and in compliance with state law. It is also the process of legally settling one's estate, a process which, without a valid will, can be a lengthy ordeal in terms of time and money.

Recipient—the individual who is receiving Medicaid.

Skilled-care facility—a facility which provides intense, comprehensive, and frequent nursing care and services, under the direction of a physician. Care is provided 24 hours a day, seven days a week, by licensed personnel under the supervision of a registered nurse.

There are some nursing home facilities which are neither skilled nor intermediate, and these nursing homes are usually referred to as custodial nursing homes and they do not participate in Medicaid.

Spend down—the process of liquidating one's assets and disposing of one's finances preferably through the payment of medical bills, until one reaches the acceptable limit for medical eligibility. This also applies when one's income exceeds the standard used for automatic Medicaid eligibility; he or she may still become eligible if he or she has incurred sufficient out-of-pocket medical expenses.

SSI—the federal Supplemental Security Income program available to persons 65 years of age and over, or to blind or disabled persons whose income and resources are below specified levels. Persons 65 years of age and over who are receiving SSI are almost always immediately eligible for Medicaid.

APPENDIX

The current population in the United States that is over 65 years of age is 29.8 million, as of July 1, 1987. That part of the U.S. population that is over 85 years of age is 2.8 million.[1] It is estimated that approximately 1.5 million people will enter nursing homes within the next five years.

For life expectancy in the United States, see the table on the following page.

---

[1] These are the most recent government figures available.

LIFE EXPECTANCY AT BIRTH AND AGE 65 BY RACE AND SEX: 1900–1985

Year	All Races Both Sexes	All Races Male	All Races Female	White Both Sexes	White Male	White Female	Black Both Sexes	Black Male	Black Female
At Birth:									
1900[1,2]	47.3	46.3	48.3	47.6	46.6	48.7	33.0[3]	32.5[3]	33.5[3]
1950[2]	68.2	65.6	71.1	69.1	66.5	72.2	60.7	58.9	62.7
1960[2]	69.7	66.6	73.1	70.6	67.4	74.1	63.2	60.7	65.9
1970	70.9	67.1	74.8	71.7	68.0	75.6	64.1	60.0	68.3
1980	73.7	70.0	77.4	74.4	70.7	78.1	68.1	63.8	72.5
1985[2,4]	74.7	71.2	78.2	75.3	71.8	78.7	69.5	65.3	73.7
At Age 65:									
1900-02[1,2]	11.9	11.5	12.2	—	11.5	12.2	—	10.4[3]	11.4[3]
1950[2]	13.9	12.8	15.0	—	12.8	15.1	13.9	12.9	14.9
1960[2]	14.3	12.8	15.8	14.4	12.9	15.9	13.9	12.7	15.1
1970	15.2	13.1	17.0	15.2	13.1	17.1	14.2	12.5	15.7
1980	16.4	14.1	18.3	16.5	14.2	18.4	15.1	13.0	16.8
1985[2,4]	16.8	14.6	18.6	16.8	14.6	18.7	15.5	13.3	17.2

SOURCE: National Center for Health Statistics, *Health, United States, 1985* DHHS Pub. No PHS 87-1232, Washington, DC: Department of Health and Human Services, December 1986.

[1] Ten states and the District of Columbia.
[2] Includes deaths of nonresidents of the United States.
[3] Figure is for the nonwhite population.
[4] Provisional data.

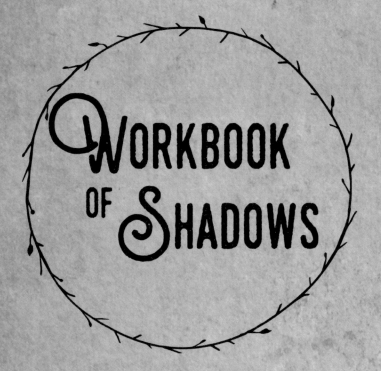

Workbook of Shadows

A Simple Guide for Beginning Wiccans

This edition first published in 2017 by
Raven in a World Tree

Copyright © 2017 by Daniel Blackthorn and Susan Landsman

All rights reserved. No part of this publication may be reproduced or transmitted in any form or by any means, without permission in writing from Raven In A World Tree. Reviewers may quote brief passages.

This book is dedicated to the Goddess Danu,
and to You, the New Wiccan.

HOW TO USE THIS BOOK

So, you have discovered Wicca! You have discovered a 'no faith required' religion where everything is based on reality. This can be a wonderful time and the beginning of a lifelong path.

Many who discover Wicca are elated and very excited to finally have found a religion that speaks to them. But very often, the beginning can be overwhelming. It's so easy to keep reading books and looking for tools and asking questions, so that you never end up getting around to actually practicing Wicca.

That is where this book can help you. This workbook will walk you along from the first steps and beginning concepts to performing a ritual and writing spells. After a short time you will be a practicing Wiccan. You will develop a basic competence and a feeling of confidence. You will be empowered to move forward in your own path.

Work through this book in order, reading the basic information and thinking about what it means to you. The journaling sections that follow are really where you make this book yours. There are pages at the end of the book for additional notes. You can use this to add information you come across as you progress, or cut and paste altar ideas or spells you come across and want to keep.

Eventually you will want to create your own Book of Shadows. In the meantime, we intend that you can use this book as your first Book of Shadows.

Enjoy the journey, and Blessed Be!

- Sue and Daniel
- Raven In A World Tree

Contents

WICCA IN A NUTSHELL 8

THE TOOLS OF A WICCAN 12

SACRED SPACE 16

YOUR ALTAR 20

THE ELEMENTS 24

THE SABBATS (THE WHEEL OF THE YEAR) 28

THE ESBATS (MOON CYCLES) 32

MEDITATION 36

SPELLS 42

RITUAL 48

DEDICATION AND INITIATION 52

THE WICCAN REDE 53

MAKING A BOOK OF SHADOWS 54

YOUR BOOK OF SHADOWS 55

WICCA IN A NUTSHELL

Wicca is a beautiful religion that many are finding fits them perfectly. The simplest definition of Wicca is Witchcraft with attention to Goddesses and Gods. There are many ways to approach the craft, and many Goddesses and Gods from different times and cultures. You will discover what appeals to you, but you do not need to know this to start.

Many who discover Wicca feel like they have come home. The excitement can be wonderful! You may feel like yelling it from the roof, but find you need to keep silent because other people will not understand. Despite this, enjoy this excitement. There is nothing greater than finding your path.

In Wicca we observe nature--both that of Earth, and of ourselves. As Wiccans we believe we are powerful individuals that can influence and create the reality around us. We do magick to improve our lives and those around us.

Wiccans often choose one pantheon -- a group of Goddesses/Gods from a certain time and region, such as Celtic, or Egyptian. Others pull from many pantheons as they feel called. This is all up to you. It may be based on your heritage, or just something you are drawn to. To start, "God" and "Goddess" are just fine.

Wiccans celebrate eight holidays called Sabbats, which are the solar holidays that coincide with the four seasons and the halfway point between each season. Wiccans also celebrate the lunar cycles, honoring the moon and its phases as Esbats. It can be such a wonderful feeling to celebrate holidays that are anchored in a reality you can see around you.

Choosing how you do things is your own Wiccan path. Let's brainstorm a little about where you are now and what you like.

What appeals to you about Wicca?
- Celebrating nature and the wheel of the year
- Witchcraft
- The Gods and Goddess'
- Fae
- Spirituality

What cultures and pantheons are you drawn to?
- Celtic
- Hindu
- Buddahism

What holidays and times of year are you drawn to celebrate?

I love fall and christmas season

What do you need more of in your life?

What times of year energize you, are ripe for projects, or make you want to hide inside and do inner work?

THE TOOLS OF A WICCAN

It can be so tempting in the beginning to spend hours at all the pagan stores around you or to hunt online for the tools you need, and spend all your time shopping instead of getting around to doing anything. It's also easy to feel like you can't do any ritual work before you have every single tool you might need -- which can make you feel too overwhelmed to start, and can dampen your enthusiasm.

It is important to realize that the tools for the most part are simply aids to directing your focus. They make your practice personal and fun, but they're not necessary to start with and can often make a ritual overly complicated for a beginner. Not to mention, you shouldn't need to spend a lot of money just to start practicing.

By all means, use whatever tools you wish. You can easily substitute "proper" tools with what you have on hand until you find the right ones, or you can use our Wiccan Toolkit™, available at our website.

Be sure to take your time in your search for tools. You want to really feel an attachment to each tool. Enjoy the experience of the search and let the right tools find you. You will likely want to cleanse your tools with incense or smudge after you get them, and dedicate them to your work in a special ritual.

You may also need to take into account your living arrangements when you buy tools, and how you plan to store them.

On the next few pages we will help you figure out what will work for you.

The tools you may want are:

Wand - A long object, often made of wood or stone, or combination of both, used to direct energy gently. If you don't have one, you can use your finger.

Athame - A ceremonial blade used to direct energy in a strong manner. If you don't have one, you can use your finger, or a stick.

Cauldron - A cast iron vessel used to burn herbs or for other ritual use. You can use an incense burner instead.

Candles - Use four candles to invoke the elements, or for specific blessings. You can use symbols, stones, or just mark the compass directions somehow. Use other candles to represent the God, Goddess, or Spirit. If you are worried about fire or cannot use candles where you are, you can use stones or other symbolic items.

A lighter - You want something reliable and safe. A butane lighter with a long neck is good for candles that often burn down on the inside leaving hard-to-reach wicks.

A snuffer - Many people believe that it is disrespectful to blow out your candles, especially those of the God and Goddess. If you don't have one, don't worry about it.

Boline - A knife, used for cutting things. You can use a kitchen knife as a simple substitute for this.

Chalice - A nice cup, used for water blessed by the Goddess.

Smudge - A wrapped stick of sage or other herbs, used to clear space regularly, or before a ritual. You will also want a dish to catch the embers from your smudge and help you put it out.

What's your style? Do you want your work to be simple and uncluttered, or do you like a lot of ritual and special setting?

How do the logistics of your living situation affect what or how many tools you might want?

What do you already have that you could use for your ritual work?

Poke around on the internet for tools. What attracts you?

SACRED SPACE

The most important thing about devoting yourself to a new spiritual path is giving yourself the space to do so. This means honoring your new path by making special areas in your environment and honored time in your schedule.

Sacred space doesn't have to be fancy. It just needs to be something you create with the intention to give yourself a comfortable and uninterrupted place to study, reflect, meditate, or conduct rituals. This could be one place, or many.

The idea of sacred space is that it helps get you into the mindset of doing your spiritual work. We get so busy in our daily lives that it's hard to shift gears, and often our spiritual life falls by the wayside. Your space will remind you to pursue your goals, and it will welcome and relax you so that you can ease away from the stress of your daily life and be in a "time away from time."

Of course, the space you create will depend on your environment. If you share space with others, you may just want to use a special candle and placemat that you can pull out whenever you are doing your work. You can use a tray stored under your bed, or a small shelf on a wall.

If you feel like you have to hide your Wiccan ways, you can still create sacred space with natural items and a few inspirational pictures that will not look overtly religious but still inspire and motivate you.

If you are fortunate enough to live on your own or have understanding roommates or family, you can be more flexible and open.

Look around your space and figure out how you could make it more "sacred" to you.

Do you need to factor other people into your setup? How could you do this?

What kind of things make you feel relaxed and help you focus?

How can you make your space different from the rest of your environment?

Do you like to change your space with the seasons? What are ways you can do this?

Do you want to incorporate any Gods or Goddesses in your space? How can you do so?

YOUR ALTAR

An altar is a crucial part of your sacred space. It is a small space specifically dedicated to a certain type of work or worship. You may have only one altar, or several altars dedicated to specific deities or for divination or meditation.

Setting up your altar can be quite fun and exciting, no matter what it looks like in the beginning. If you are like most of us in the beginning you have almost nothing. That's ok, and sometimes simpler is better.

The location of your altar is important. It should be someplace where you can see it, and where it is comfortable for you to sit. If you are somewhere where you can do rituals outside you can do that too. Of course, you will want your altar in a place that has some privacy and quiet.

If you have neither in a permanent setup, create a portable altar and just go with the flow. We've done rituals in a locked bathroom for lack of a better space! Obviously this is not ideal, but in reality, anywhere is good in the beginning.

If you are using your altar for ritual, the directions relative to the area are important. You should mark in some way where North, South, East and West are so you don't have to think about it during ritual.

Do you want more than one altar?

What items are special to you that you want to put on your altar?

What do you intend to do at your altar or altars?

Find examples of other people's altars -- what do you like about them? What don't you like?

THE ELEMENTS

The Elements are a very important part of Wicca for meditation and learning, for spell casting, and for ritual.

Each element (Earth, Air, Water, and Fire) is represented by Elemental beings from the astral plane. This can be studied later in your journey. For now, we only need to use the elements for focus of energy. Here are some associations to start with:

AIR: Creativity, Intelligence, Inspiration, Ideas, East
Yellow
Aroma, the Wand, Wind, Smoke from incense

WATER: Emotions, Wisdom, West
Blue
Holy water, Washing, the Chalice

FIRE: Forceful energy, Inspiration, Passion, Love, South
Red
Candles, Incense, Burnings

EARTH: Manifestation, Strength, Prosperity, Stability, North
Green
Dirt, Wood, Stone, Herbs, Pentacle

SPIRIT: Provides balance for all of the Elements
White, Purple
a Goddess Statue, or any special object

There are many different associations for the elements. Be sure to use what you feel is right for you. For example, if you live on the East Coast of the US you might want water to be East. Do as you see fit.

Where are the directions relative to you, in your house or apartment?

What associations do you have with Air?

What associations do you have with Fire?

What associations do you have with Water?

What associations do you have with Earth?

What tools or items represent these things to you in a way that's personal and meaningful?

THE SABBATS (THE WHEEL OF THE YEAR)

The sabbats are a very wonderful part of being Wiccan. They mark the four seasons and the four halfway points between the seasons. It is common to find Wiccans following the seasonal wheel of the ancient Celtic culture.

You will see so many ideas, stories, rocks, herbs, colors, gods, and goddesses associated with each Sabbat that it can be overwhelming. Some will try to argue that the ancients or their own group or coven does things The Right Way. You need to ignore this and do what works for you.

Each culture in the past came up with their correspondences based on their environment, culture, and how they viewed their world. But what do you do if you follow the Celtic Sabbats but you live in the Southern Hemisphere and your seasons are exactly opposite? You need to choose your own correspondences for the Sabbats based on where you live and what makes sense to you, just as you will pick your deities, your prayers, and your intentions.

For now, it could be enough to simply acknowledge the time of year and the energies you feel at the Sabbats. It can be nice to do a ritual for the Sabbat consisting simply of a meditation focusing on the time of year and all that it means to you.

Many Wiccans like to start the year with Samhain because the next day is the Celtic new year. If you follow another culture's wheel of the year, you will find variations. Eventually you will pick what resonates with you.

The energies of the Sabbats can be felt days before and days after so don't worry too much about doing a ritual on the exact date of the Sabbat. Very often life interferes!

SAMHAIN - OCTOBER 31
(SOW-en) Half way between Autumn and Winter.

YULE - DECEMBER 20, 21, 22, OR 23
(yool) The beginning of Winter.

IMBOLC - FEBRUARY 1 OR 2
(imb-OLC) Half way between Winter and Spring.

OSTARA - MARCH 20, 21, 22, OR 23
(O-Star-a) The beginning of Spring.

BELTANE - APRIL 30 OR MAY 1
(BEL-tane) Half way between Spring and Summer.

LITHA - JUNE 20, 21, 22, OR 23
(LEE-tha) The beginning of Summer.

LUGHNASADH - AUGUST 1
(loo-NOSS-ah) Half way between Summer and Autumn.

MABON - SEPTEMBER 20, 21, 22, OR 23
(MAY-bon) The beginning of Autumn.

The sabbats mark important points in the year. What are the important points for you?

Going with the Celtic system for now, write down what is meaningful to you about these sabbats and times of year.

How do you like to celebrate the passing of time?

How does the wheel of the year work with your own energies? Are you busy in Summer and introverted in winter? The other way around?

THE ESBATS (MOON CYCLES)

Following the moon phases is one of a Wiccan's favorite things to do, because we feel the energy of full and new and everything in between. Especially when we give the moon our attention, we can understand how our own cycles correlate with the cycles of nature in a time that's short enough to perceive and work with.

Try to see and think about the moon often, try to learn where and why it looks like it does in its different phases. The energies of the moon can give our spells and rituals more power. The relationship of the Earth and Moon can seem complicated, but it's easy to find a grade-school science explanation on the internet. Give the Earth/Moon relationship your attention and you will come to understand it better and you will learn how to use its energy for your meditations and spells.

The New Moon marks the beginning of the lunar cycle. This is a time for inner reflection, and perhaps setting new intentions. You might do a New Moon ritual for setting a short term goal for youself. Or, you might do a meditation within a ritual in order to contact the New Moon Goddess (Crone) or God (Sage) in a search for wisdom.

The Full Moon is the peak of the lunar cycle and is a time of manifesting what you have been focused on over the past month. For now, you might do a Full Moon ritual where you thank Goddess, God, and the Universe for what you have. The moon cycles pass quickly, so don't worry, you will have many more in which to do more advanced magick.

Working with the moon and its many phases can be complicated, but it doesn't have to be to start out. Just pay attention, experiment, and write things down.

Over the next month or so, see how the phases of the moon manifest where you are. Where is the full moon? Where is the new moon? Draw pictures:

How does your mood vary with the cycles of the moon? Jot down a word or a rating between 1 and 10 daily, and see how it corresponds. Trying this for several months will give you more information.

The moon cycle is a good way to put a framework on your spiritual practice. What could you do within the frame of a month?

The moon cycle is about setting new intentions, doing the work to manifest them, harvesting your work, and releasing what didn't grow. What are ways you can do this that are meaningful to you?

MEDITATION

Meditation is a very important part of being Wiccan because it brings you to a quiet place inside where you can connect with your inner knowledge or your spiritual guides. This is also the place where you generate power for your spells and rituals.

There are many resources and guided meditations available. Our goal is to give you some practice right away with some progressively difficult forms of meditation. Try each one several times and journal your results on the pages that follow.

In all three meditations, start by getting very comfortable. Clothing, room temperature, and space are important.

BEGINNING MEDITATION

Sit and breathe evenly and think about how nice it is to relax. Either close your eyes or light a candle and watch the flame with relaxed eyes. Try and clear your mind. As thoughts come into your mind just gently acknowledge them and let them go. Do this for five minutes to start and increase time as you wish.

INNER MEDITATION:

In this type of meditation you will simply look within yourself for information about yourself. Be forgiving of yourself if need be and realize that you are an important part of the Universe. You are connected to it and completely within it.

Start with the beginning meditation and then, when you have cultivated the empty space, ask yourself "What do I need to know right now?" and see what comes into that space. You can also meditate with the intention of discovering something about yourself by following the thoughts and images that come to you.

One experiment you might try is to take yourself back to when you were born, before parents and society intervened in who you are. See if you can feel what and who you were at birth.

OUTER MEDITATION:

In this type of meditation you will be taking yourself on a journey to seek wisdom from outside yourself.

Start with the beginning meditation and then, when you have cultivated the empty space, imagine and visualize a stone walkway leading into an area that has two pathways. One path leads to the left, and one to the right. Before the paths is a small grassy area and some benches where you may sit for a bit if you would like.

Both paths lead in different directions into a forest.

Choose a path when you feel stronger about one more than the other.

Start walking down the path and notice any details you may see. Eventually you will come to some sort of structure. When the time is right, your spirit guide will meet you inside. If you do not meet a guide, just be present; it may take a few times before your guide is ready to appear. When you are ready to leave, express your gratitude, follow the path back, and slowly return to yourself.

You can use this meditation format to find your God and Goddess guides, find your Wiccan Name, or seek wisdom from whoever is there to offer it.

Use the following pages to record your experiences with these meditations. You'll want to practice the beginning meditation many times and the others at least twice.

BEGINNING MEDITATION 1:

BEGINNING MEDITATION 2:

INNER MEDITATION 1:

INNER MEDITATION 2:

INNER MEDITATION 3:

OUTER MEDITATION 1:

OUTER MEDITATION 2:

OUTER MEDITATION 3:

SPELLS

A spell is a way to use your power to manifest a result in your environment. You must be very specific and careful when you do this, and never use your power to manipulate someone else.

The steps in writing a spell are on the next page. After that, there is a sample spell, then three pages for you to write your own practice spells and record the results.

Writing and casting a spell is a process that involves the Wiccan precepts of *To Know*, *To Dare*, *To Will*, and *To Be Silent*.

Know exactly what you want, *Dare* to ask for it without doubt, *Will* its manifestation with your power, and then *Be Silent*, which means don't dissipate your power by telling people about it or asking the universe over and over again.

When casting a spell in ritual, you can call upon one or more of the Elements for their energies. Here are some associations for the elements that you can use:

Air: creativity, intent - to Know

Water: communication - to Dare

Fire: forceful energy - to Will

Earth: manifestation - to be Silent

After you have cast a spell, be sure to write down any thoughts and feelings about the experience of casting the spell, and leave space for writing down any results later. Also, be sure to help manifest what it is you asked for by creating ways in your life for it to manifest. Remember, you have power, so use it.

We have given you space to practice writing three spells. Don't forget to record your results later!

STEPS IN SPELLCRAFTING

INTENTION: Obviously, there's a reason you want to write a spell. Usually people identify a lack of something, or something in their life they want less of. Keep your state of mind positive about the spell. Know that it will work, and that the results will be for the highest good. (Example: I need more money!)

FOCUS: The focus refines your intention into something that manifests exactly what will help you. You want to be very specific about what the spell is for. It must be focused. You should be able to state what you want in very few words. (Example: I want funds to pay my bills for this month.)

WRITE YOUR SPELL: You can find a spell that works for you, but it's always better to write your own so that you know the words are right. Write it down so you can read it during ritual. Many people prefer rhyme to make it easier to remember and because it sounds cool, but do what works for you. It helps to end with something like "This or better, for my highest good" (Example: "Please let it come in any way/ the funds this month my bills to pay./ This or better for my highest good."

CAST YOUR SPELL: The purpose of the ritual is to raise the energy from the Elements by visualizing each of the energies contributing to your intent. Direct the energy and intent to the Universe, cast your spell out loud, and release it by either saying 'So mote it be!' with strength and resolve, or stomping the ground saying 'It is done!', or any such thing. If you wish, you can also include some symbol or item that represents your desire that you can later put on your altar.

SAMPLE SPELL:

INTENT: I'm having trouble sleeping. I'm tired all the time and want more energy.

FOCUS: I'd like to wake up in the morning feeling rested and have enough energy to make it through the day.

THE SPELL:

When time to rise I will awake

with zest and power for the full day.

I will not tire till time to sleep,

Then fully relaxed, I'll hit the hay.

This or better for my highest good,

So mote it be.

NOTES AND RESULTS: This worked really well for two days, then I felt tired again. Maybe I should rewrite the spell to work for a week, or cast it more often!

SPELL NAME:
INTENT:

FOCUS:

THE SPELL:

NOTES AND RESULTS:

SPELL NAME:
INTENT:

FOCUS:

THE SPELL:

NOTES AND RESULTS:

SPELL NAME:
INTENT:

FOCUS:

THE SPELL:

NOTES AND RESULTS:

RITUAL

A ritual is a stage for invoking energy and focusing your own intent in order to accomplish a particular goal. It could be simply honoring the phase of the moon, or could be done for releasing a limiting belief, requesting the presence of a spirit or deity, or casting a spell.

Rituals usually have a specific order, though the complexity of each step will vary depending on the person. Our goal is to provide you with a basic ritual for you to practice with. Ideally, you will perform this ritual several times, perhaps with a different purpose each time. Having done this, it will be easier for you to experiment with what works for you and customize your own ritual.

Some prefer a quick, simple meditation before starting a ritual. This could be just five minutes where you simply sit and clear your mind of any events of the day. You don't have to completely clear everything out, the point is to just relax. Sometimes meditative music is nice to have before and during a ritual.

The first thing you will want to do is to gather up all the tools you want for your ritual. Remember that you are really the power and the tools are simply to help you focus. If you don't have a tool, improvise with some of the substitutions we recommended, or use your Wiccan Toolkit© so you can practice without worrying about whether you have everything.

The next page describes the ritual order and the purpose of the different components. The following pages contain a simple ritual, with invocations, for you to use as a practice ritual. As you become experienced, you will want to substitute your own wordings and processes.

CLEARING YOUR SPACE
This is a way of clearing stale energy out of your sacred space. Use your smudge, or you can use a bell or clap your hands.

CASTING THE CIRCLE:
The circle is a protected area around you that you cast before ritual. It is actually a sphere surrounding you and your ritual space. Go round the circle with an index finger or wand three times chanting the circle words. You can start with what is here, make your own, or search other sources for what you prefer.

INVOKING THE ELEMENTS:
In order to perform the work we're doing in our ritual it helps to have the assistance of the elemental beings of Earth, Air, Fire, and Water. You may want to light their candles as you do so.

INVOKING THE DEITY:
It also helps to call on the presence of the God and or Goddess. You can also just call upon Spirit or whatever you choose.

CONDUCTING YOUR RITUAL WORK:
You should have a purpose, whether it be dedicating your tools, performing a meditation, or casting a spell.

THANK THE DEITY AND THE ELEMENTS::
Since you have summoned the presence of deity and the elemental beings, you must thank and release them. This would be the time to snuff their candles.

OPEN THE CIRCLE:
At the end of the ritual, you must release the energy and protection you have created.

RAVEN IN A WORLD TREE WICCAN RITUAL

CLEAR YOUR SPACE:

Use your smudge to clear the energy of your space. Or, you can use a bell or clap your hands.

CAST THE CIRCLE:

Starting at the North, go around the circle three times deosil (clockwise), saying one verse each time as you pass the elements from Earth to Air, to Fire then Water.

First time around, holding your athame, wand, or a substitute:

> "I draw this circle round me,
> each time with more power,
> bring me thus between the worlds,
> in this magikal hour."

Second time around, sprinkling water from the chalice.

> "Manifestations from Earth,
> things of the mind from Air,
> passion and drive from Fire,
> and wisdom from Water so fair."

Third time around, bringing your incense around the circle (if you are using the Wiccan Toolkit©, use the smudge card again.)

> "Welcome spirits of the ages,
> For wisdom Crones and Sages
> now my powers be revealed,
> I claim this Circle to be sealed!"

INVOKE THE ELEMENTS:

Light a candle if you wish. Call upon the Elementals (creatures of the Astral Plane) in each elemental direction. Stand in the center of your circle and face each direction as you say the words:

Earth, North: "Welcome Elementals of Earth! Come lend your energies of manifestation and form if you please."

Air, East: "Welcome Elementals of Air! Come lend your energies of creativity and inspiration if you please."

Fire, South: "Welcome Elementals of Fire! Come lend your energies of passion and motivation if you please."

Water, West: "Welcome Elementals of Water! Come lend your energies of wisdom and peace if you please."

INVOKE THE DEITY:

Call upon your version of deity or spirit as you wish.

CONDUCT YOUR RIITUAL WORK:

Now sit in the circle and be present with the energy. When you feel ready, perform your ritual work, meditation, or spell.

THANK THE DEITY AND THE ELEMENTS:

"I thank you (God/Goddess), for your constant presence."
"I thank you Elementals of the (Direction), until we meet again."
(for each direction of West, South, East, and North)

OPEN THE CIRCLE:

Now open the circle with your index finger, wand, or a substitute, starting in the West and moving around widdershins (counter-clockwise). You will bring up the energy through the tool you are using into yourself. Begin by saying:

"Blessed Be the power in me! I am thankful for all there is. I now declare my circle open and its protection stays with me."

Now tap your hands on the floor, or stomp your feet, to drain the energy you absorbed back into the Earth.

DEDICATION AND INITIATION

When you become very sure that you are on the right path with Wicca you may feel you want to do a dedication to the craft, either alone or with others.

For this, check some books and look online for different dedication rituals. You can modify the ones you find to suit you, or write your own. There is no rush. Be sure you are ready, because this is a lifetime dedication to your Goddess or God and to your religion. Obvioulsly, you can change your mind later, but the seriousness of the commitment should be there.

Initiation happens when you find a Coven and they agree to let you join. This should be a beautiful and comfortable ritual. If anyone tries to pressure you into doing something you are not comfortable with, then it is the wrong Coven. Don't worry, being a solitary witch is a beautiful and powerful way to go until you find the right Coven. Many people also prefer to practice solitary and associate with others in a purely social manner.

Before you dedicate yourself, you should understand the basic code of ethics as described in the Wiccan Rede.

THE WICCAN REDE

The Wiccan Rede is the main moral system for Wicca. 'Rede' means advice. The eight words shown below give us a lot to watch out for. Harming none can be a little tricky, so be careful in the spells you do and in what you wish for.

Eight words the Wiccan Rede fulfill:
An ye harm none, do what ye will.

There are several long versions of the rede that can be found online and in books. The long version is fun to read, but these eight words remain the most important.

MAKING A BOOK OF SHADOWS

Most Wiccans end up keeping a journal of their work, discoveries, and reference material in something called a "Book of Shadows." This is usually an ongoing effort that develops over the course of a lifetime. People have different preferences for what they use, and most people end up experimenting, using multiple books, or changing from one to another over time. The main point of the book is to have a place to put all your important Wiccan findings. Here are some possibilities for you to consider.

THREE-RING BINDER
This works really well if you print a lot of information off the internet, or photocopy a lot of material from books. It also makes it easy to put your book in sections and reorganize your papers as you add new things or decide you no longer want something in there.

FANCY JOURNAL
These look great, and are wonderful to hold. This can be a good choice for material which you know you will want to keep long term, or if you're intending to pass the journal on to your offspring.

MOLESKINES
Moleskine notebooks make good "working" notebooks that can also be used to organize your material. You can use one for spells, one for rituals, and another to log your current practice, switching it out as time goes by.

ONLINE
If you prefer to keep your material organized online instead of an actual book, you can use a system such as Evernote to file your material with the appropriate tags and means of identification. This makes searching your material easy.

YOUR BOOK OF SHADOWS

Raven in a World Tree

is

Daniel Blackthorn and Sue Landsman,
who share a home and a desire to help new
Wiccans find their own path and experienced
ones better integrate their spirituality into
their daily lives.

Please check out our blog and our other
products on our web site at
http://www.raveninaworldtree.com

Our other books:
Workbook of Sabbats
Workbook of Tarot
Workbook of the Moon

Blessed be.